FOREIGN POLICY MAKING IN COMMUNIST COUNTRIES

Edited by
HANNES ADOMEIT
ROBERT BOARDMAN

Foreign Policy Making in Communist Countries

A Comparative Approach

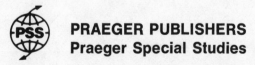

PRAEGER PUBLISHERS
Praeger Special Studies

New York • London • Sydney • Toronto

PRAEGER PUBLISHERS, PRAEGER SPECIAL STUDIES
383 Madison Avenue, New York, N.Y. 10017, U.S.A.

Published in the United States of America in 1979
by Praeger Publishers
A Division of Holt, Rinehart and Winston, CBS, Inc.

© 1979 by H. Adomeit and R. Boardman

Library of Congress Catalog Card Number: 78-70493

Printed in Great Britain

Contents

The contributors

Hannes Adomeit   Lecturer in Soviet foreign policy, Institute for Soviet and East European Studies, University of Glasgow. 1977-79, study leave at the Centre for International Relations, Queen's University, Kingston, Ontario.

Robert Boardman   Associate Professor Department of Political Science, Dalhousie University, Nova Scotia.

Jeanne Kirk Laux   Associate Professor, Department of Political Science, University of Ottawa.

Peter Marsh   Lecturer, Department of History, Manchester Polytechnic.

Preface

Authors can usually be relied upon to think of good reasons why their books should be published. So can the editors of anthologies, especially it seems in the social sciences. It happens less often that such collections break much new and useful ground; sometimes they merely testify to the editor's inventiveness in finding a common denominator vague enough to accommodate diversity yet specific enough not to offend scientific propriety. We hope, however, that we are justified in making a modest claim of relevance for the present volume by adopting and exploring a comparative approach to the study of communist foreign policies, and foreign policy making in particular.

The usefulness of the exercise is enhanced by the fact that it is part of a three-volume series of the comparative analysis of foreign policy making, under the general editorship of William Wallace. (The other two volumes examine the making of foreign policy in Western Europe and in the developing countries, and are edited respectively by W. Paterson and William Wallace, and by Christopher Clapham.) The overall purpose of the series is to combine an informative and empirical analysis of foreign policy making in various regions with an awareness of the theoretical approaches to the subject, and to illuminate such similarities and differences as may exist between countries of different socio-economic and political structure in the sphere of foreign policy making.

In their introductory essay the editors discuss the problems and potential value of concepts developed in the theoretical literature on foreign policy for the study of communist states. They argue that while some approaches my bear too indelibly the imprint of the Western setting where they almost invariably originated, it would nevertheless be unwise to discard as inappropriate or inapplicable the full range and diversity of recent theorising. The main part of the book focuses on foreign policy making in the two largest communist powers, the Soviet Union and China, as well as on two countries in the Soviet sphere of influence where the 'Soviet experience' has been transplanted — Romania and East Germany. While working within the same general framework, each author has made his or her own judgment about the relative importance of the different factors involved in foreign policy making in 'their' countries. In the concluding chapter the editors reconsider the questions raised at the beginning. Drawing on the material presented in the book, they attempt to derive some generalisations and point out different paths along which the comparative study of communist foreign policy might fruitfully be pursued.

We should like to express thanks to the Political Studies Association at whose Annual Conference some years ago (in 1974 in Lancaster) the idea for the present series first took shape; to many friends and colleagues with whom the project and individual contributions have been discussed; and particularly to Mr John Irwin of Teakfield, Ltd, without whose encouragement and support this series would not have been possible.

July 1978

William Wallace
Royal Institute of International Affairs

Hannes Adomeit
University of Glasgow and Centre for International Relations, Queen's University, Kingston, Ontario

Robert Boardman
Dalhousie University

1 The comparative study of communist foreign policy.

HANNES ADOMEIT AND ROBERT BOARDMAN

The prolific literature on comparative communism indicates some measure of agreement about the structural foundations of the field of enquiry. In fact, one can derive from this literature the proposition that there is a communist research system, whose members share similar institutions, standards and values,[1] and that it is possible to use these in a comparative approach to the study of communist foreign policies and foreign policy making. However, disagreements about fairly important research problems do divide scholars. Some of these questions can be put as follows: what are the constraints and opportunities derived from dependence, autonomy or dominance in the alliance system and within the 'international communist movement'? What is the relationship between Party and state, and how meaningful is it to assume a dichotomy between the two? How high is the degree of centralisation and consensus in foreign policy making as opposed to the influence of 'bureaucratic politics', 'organizational processes', 'power struggle' or 'interest groups'? More specifically, what is the role of the military in shaping foreign policy, including policy on questions of arms control and in international crises (especially important in the study of the USSR and China); and what is the respective influence of the 'technocrats' and economic managers *vis-à-vis* the Party on issues of international economic cooperation and détente? Finally, to take further this 'red' versus 'expert' dichotomy, what (if any) is the role of Marxist-Leninist ideology, 'instrumental beliefs' or *Weltanschauung* in shaping the behaviour, and perhaps even the 'operational principles', of the political leaders in communist countries?

These questions are important enough to be asked in the study of the foreign policy of each individual communist country, and they might as well be asked in comparative perspective. The tool of comparison, however, has not usually been applied systematically. It has been perhaps more evident in pedagogy than in scholarship. In research, it has been more implied than consciously used. General notions, not always articulated, about the character of communist systems have informed research strategies, suggested case studies, and assisted between the lines interpretations of documents. But change has become a feature of communist studies. Criticisms of the failure of communist studies to launch themselves into something vaguely identified as a 'mainstream' of social science have multiplied, and explorations abound of what a discipline of comparative communist politics should or should not look like.[2] As a result it has become almost impossible for a paper to be published on, say, Czechoslovakia,[3] Romania,[4] or East Germany,[5] without its author first drawing attention to the inability of 'the totalitarian model' to cope with the complexity of his subject. It has seemed (and in our view is) ill fitted to the task of explaining change because of its undue emphasis on the role of regime coercion, its characteristic approach to questions of legitimacy and its neglect of the sheer variety of political relationships present in any political system.

Linked to the depreciation of the totalitarian model is the increasingly widespread theme of the 'erosion' or 'end of ideology' in communist politics, the idea that ideology can no longer be considered as having analytical, mobilising or motivating functions (*Antriebsideologie*) but that it has merely a ritualistic and legitimising quality (*Rechtfertigungsideologie*) and hence is only of marginal importance for policy making. Tendentially, this kind of reasoning had always appealed to the Western analyst. To scholars reared in the Anglo-Saxon tradition of empiricism and pragmatism, the very thought that leaders in the 'practical' realm of politics in the twentieth century could or should be guided in their actions by a 'rigid' belief system has appeared implausible. They have found the Hegelian form of ideology, as embodied in the ruling communist parties, difficult to grasp, and their (the parties') pronouncements 'appear to them similar to the chants and litanies of some esoteric religious cult.'[6]

This basic philosophical preconditioning has been reinforced recently by the 'behavioural revolution' in the social sciences with its generation of pressures, often justified, for more stringent measurement and higher standards of verification. But there are tremendous problems of, as the jargon has it, 'operationalising' a research problem such as the influence of ideology in policy making. As a result it often appears more appropriate to delete a factor such as ideology altogether rather than open the research design to the charge of being 'unscientific'. Ideology, therefore, is often being more eroded by default than design.

Changes in trends and fashion in the last decade have included also a debasement of area studies as a reactionary approach that stands in the way of progress and precision. Unfortunately, it has not always been

2

clear what is meant by the 'scientific approach'. To some it is a call to interdisciplinary endeavour (which misses the point because the core of area studies has always been its integrative focus on the historical, cultural, ideological, geographical, economic, military and political factors considered to be specific to one particular country or area); to others it is an exhortation to grand theorising and model building, which is questionable advice given the deficiencies in the state of the art; finally, and with much greater justification, it can be taken to mean greater conceptual awareness, openness to the possibilities of comparison with other systems, and the realisation that there may be general patterns beyond the confines of supposedly unique features.

There has also been a related and regrettable denunciation of the historical approach. As Stephen Cohen has pointed out for Soviet studies, previously 'history and political science were often indistinguishable disciplines', but since the mid-1960s the behavioural revolution with its ahistorical and even anti-historical methodism had won over many specialists. 'Political scientists in the field no longer investigate the history and culture of the Soviet Union, much less of pre-revoluntionary Russia. Some perpetuate worn historical conceptions in the ritualistic 'historical background'. But most concentrate exclusively on contemporary 'data.'

Yet Europeans and Chinese have, so to speak, long memories. For them historical dates have deep significance (as, for instance, 1863 for the Poles and 1848 for the Hungarians), historical parallels are drawn (say, between 1938 and 1968 by the Czechs), and as a consequence historical symbolism takes on important contemporary political significance (as, for instance, the teachings of Confucius in China or the question of how Jan Masaryk came to fall from an office window in Prague in 1948 for Czechs and Slovaks). Almost every major dispute, from economics, culture, science, to foreign policy and the role of the Party, has been associated with historical precedent and has been full of conflicting historical symbols and allusions by rival political groups in officialdom.[9] To that extent it is wise to accept the aphorism, 'The past is never dead. It's not even past.'[10]

Other changes that have occurred in communist studies put particular emphasis on diversity of institutions, organisations and bureaucracies, diversity of social forces, and diversity of interests. Under the influence of Western organisational and group theories and the study of bureaucracy — and after the objective differentiation that has taken place in the USSR and Eastern Europe ever since Stalin's death — there is a tendency

3

among analysts to focus on conflict rather than consensus, the interplay of groups rather than centralisation, and outcomes rather than outputs.[11] Whereas previously, in an inadequate application of Max Weber, the rational and integrating functions of bureaucracy had been considered of supreme importance in communist systems, there is a realisation that Weber had considered the leaders of bureaucracies to be politicians rather than bureaucrats, and that hence, if tendentially, he had always admitted the possibility of political (or 'crypto-political') conflict at the top.[12] 'Bureaucratic politics' and 'organisational processes' hence have become part and parcel of the vocabulary of the modern analyst of communist systems. But old fashioned Kremlinology, too, with its emphasis on the perennial power struggle, and its views of political issues being mere 'pretexts' in a deadly serious game of *kto-kovo*? (Who [eliminates] whom?), has not been immune to change: the new 'conflict school' of Kremlinology has promised to be good, forget about the mistakes of the past, adopt a broad outlook and henceforth take into account the policy dimension of power struggle.[13]

These five elements, 1 the depreciation of the totalitarian model, 2 neglect of ideology, 3 disparagement of area studies, 4 denunciation of the historical approach and 5 emphasis on conflict, the interplay of groups and outcomes as distinct from output — can be considered the most important manifestations of change in communist studies. But with the exception of the first two elements the study of foreign policy of communist countries until recently had tended to resist such changes. As Horelick, Johnson and Steinbruner observed in their review of Soviet foreign policy studies, these were little affected by behaviouralist stirrings in political science in the 1960s. 'Both the extensive literature about the comparative study of Communist systems and the small body of empirical research it has inspired are oriented overwhelmingly toward the domestic politics of the Soviet Union and other Communist states. . . . The literature on Soviet foreign policy continues therefore to be overwhelmingly traditional, historical-descriptive, in character. Broad propositions about Soviet foreign policy behaviour are advanced in this literature intermittently, but not systematically. . . . There is little cumulation of comparable propositions and hypotheses.'[14]

In the case of Eastern Europe, as Bogdan Denitch has observed, there persisted the view that 'with the exception of Yugoslavia, and later Albania and Romania, there was, for all practical purposes, no such thing as a foreign policy for [these] states, and that their posture had to be understood primarily in terms of the long-range policy interests of the Soviet

Union.'[15]

In the last few years, however, change in the study of foreign policy of the communist countries has accelerated and proliferated. Some comparative studies have been done, as in Farrell's analysis of East European foreign policy leadership,[16] or Weiner's investigation of Albanian and Romanian United Nations policies.[17] Attention has been directed towards a broader range of factors, such as industrialisation and urbanisation, energy dependence, or changes in the variety of external influences,[18] in research on East European foreign policy processes. Most importantly, there has been an upsurge in attempts to explain foreign policy as a 'non-rational' resultant in the domestic parallelogram of forces (in line with the fifth element of change in communist studies mentioned above), the most notable examples to this effect being Slusser's book on Soviet-American relations in the Berlin crisis of 1961[19] and Dinerstein's book on the Cuban missile crisis.[20] Beyond that, younger scholars have begun to scrutinise the Stalin period, even the 1930s, for evidence of internal conflict affecting foreign policy.[21]

But what about the problem of comparison? On balance, one is left with the impression that research on the foreign policies of the communist countries is characterised by the same deficiencies noted a decade ago by Bernard Cohen in a general review of foreign policy studies. 'In addition to a dearth of general theories' — perhaps not such a bad thing — 'there has been very little comparative analysis in the study of foreign policy making. Rather, our analyses of institutions, individuals, and even system have been singular and for that reason not always cumulative.'[22]

Some of these issues go beyond the scope of communist studies. Complaints about lack of cumulation of insights have been made in relation to studies of British foreign policy.[23] Difficulties of applying theoretical notions arise in the case of United States foreign policy.[24] Some special problems exist, however, in the study of foreign policy and foreign policy making in communist countries.

Firstly, cultural distance, compounded by adversary relations at the inter-state level, make objective evaluations by Western observers intrinsically difficult. The divide of political values and perceptions may have been partially responsible for a focussing in research on those factors which seemed most sharply to distinguish socialist from capitalist states. The problem is perhaps universal. An anthropologist, for example, is more likely to report on phenomena in fieldwork which are different from those of his own society or subculture than he is to report on pheno-

mena common to both.[25] Cold war confronation discouraged heterogeneity in the viewpoints of scholars of Soviet or Chinese foreign
policy.[26] Hypotheses commonplace in other contexts, for example,
that perceived threat generates hostile acts, became highly controversial
when applied to Soviet or Chinese behaviour. Revisionist critiques in the
United States gave debate on east-west relations a "tis-'tisn't-'tis' flavour
hardly boding well for either historicist or social scientific progress.
Broader 'socialist'-'capitalist', Third World-communist or one-party
state - multi-party state comparisons would act to check distortions arising from an exclusive focus on communist countries.

Secondly, the existence of an international communist system has
been a retarding or complicating factor. It has encouraged far more scholarly interest in integration processes within the Soviet-East European
subsystem, or in shifting patterns of alignments within the region, than in
the foreign policies of each state, with the exception of the Soviet Union
itself. For obvious reasons, Soviet influence was taken as the predominant input into foreign policy making in the East European states, or into
that of China during the 1950s, and the degree of compliance to Soviet
wishes resulting as the sole output of significant interest.[27] Disputes
between the Soviet Union and Yugoslavia, or China, are of course
important focal points of research, as are departures from the Soviet position taken, for example, by Poland between late 1956 and early 1958,[28]
or, more characteristically, by Romania in its refusal to accept Khrushchev's plans for supranationality in Comecon in 1962 and dramatic
departures from established Warsaw Pact policy in 1967-68, including
recognition of West Germany and denunciation of its allies' military
intervention in Czechoslovakia.[29] In the respective approaches of the
Warsaw Pact member states to the German question the interests of the
Soviet Union and of individual East European countries have at times
been quite different, and not always amenable to coordinated direction
from Moscow.[30] While this, at least to some extent, had been accepted
by most observers for a number of states in Eastern Europe at various
times, the divergence of interests has also been convincingly demonstrated with regard to the USSR and the GDR.[31]

While the analysis of the degree of consensus and conflict in the Warsaw Pact, and the degree of autonomy that has at times been achieved by
various states, is definitely a fruitful line of comparative inquiry some reservations are well in place also. Too much attention to this dimension
can often obscure the view of the East European states simply as actors
engaged in the pursuit of foreign policy interests. That there exist exter-

6

nal constraints on their actions, or that on some issues these may be more exacting than for many other states in the international system, does not make them qualitatively different. At the other extreme, the apparent finality of the cleavage between Russia and China has set back scholarly interest in comparative foreign policy research spanning European and Asian communist countries. But the fact that China has embarked on a different route to socialism, and in the process engaged in a cold war confrontation with a Soviet Union dismissed by it as having reverted to capitalism, does not in itself erode the basis for comparative studies of the two countries' foreign policies.

Thirdly, comparison has been limited because of weaknesses in the general foreign policy literature. Some recent writings are still beset by the sins of the social sciences noted in 1964 by Berelson and Steiner: 'too much precision misplaced on trivial matters, too little respect for crucial facts as against grand theories, too much respect for insights that are commonplace, too much indication and too little regard for the learning of the past, far too much jargon.'[32] The onus thus comes down heavily on those arguing that behaviouralist change in communist studies would be a good change. The more traditionally minded critic is unlikely to be so persuaded by much of the 'evidence' produced by sophisticated research techniques or by exhortations to engage in grand theorising and model building.

Thus, as Arnold Horelick has noted: 'For all the talk we have heard about bringing communist studies into the mainstream of social science, the communist foreign policy field, on the plane of country studies, has barely been touched.'[33] This is underlined by Alvin Rubinstein who deplores, with justification, the fact that there are only very few exhaustively researched studies of the foreign policy of the Soviet Union, far fewer of that of China, and still fewer of Yugoslavia, Romania, Poland, Hungary, Bulgaria, East Germany, North Vietnam or North Korea. 'Far from being deluged, we suffer from a paucity of detailed, thoroughly researched, systematic treatments of the actual behaviour of these countries.'[34] Nevertheless, despite the deplorable gaps, even such an outspoken critic as Horelick acknowledges that a comparative approach would be useful if it served 'to improve and enlarge the established knowledge base about the context of foreign policy decision-making in communist countries in ways that will render that knowledge more susceptible to disciplined inquiry, and to formulate and test theories in the middle range.'[35]

Comparison, we would agree, has an important role to play in helping to remedy some of the shortcomings in the field, including lack of specificity in identifying and distinguishing those factors that are to be explained, and those that are to do the explaining, and in examining links between the two. This does not mean that one has to have a particular interest in quantitative techniques. Common sense, combined with some awareness of conceptual problems, can often be of greater help. It can also serve to avoid the temptations of what may be called 'outputism' and 'inputism', the first involving large accumulation of events and interactions of a state without attention to relevance, reasons or objectives, the second featuring detailed description of factors (such as ideology, national interests, military capabilities, economic potential, and institutions) felt somehow to be important in the determination of policy but without assessing their relative weight.[36] What would be most desirable in any comparative effort dealing with foreign policy making in communist countries is a sensible combination of traditional strategic theory with aspects of 'modern' decision theories.

Comparing the communist countries need not imply that they are similar. Indeed, it is the diversity of the socialist world, as much as any uniform elements, that points to the value of comparative research. There is huge variation in standard economic indicators. Together, Russia and China account for 85 per cent of population in the socialist states, and 75 per cent of GNP.[37] Per capita GNP ratio between the two has wavered at around 12:1, which is close to estimates of that between the developed West and the Third World (13:1). Eastern Europe, in a 'less developed' condition at the end of the Second World War, is now — intra-regional variations notwithstanding — firmly part of the Northern industrialised world. Large differences of population size encompass small countries, like Mongolia (1.4m.) and Albania (2.4m.), European states in the middle range (GDR 16.9m., Romania 21.2m., Yugoslavia 21.3m., Poland 34.0m.), and the giants of the Soviet Union (254.5m.) and China (934.6m.) There are similar variations in the attributes of economic geography. Only through comparative analysis of the foreign policies of these states can we determine satisfactorily the policy consequences of specifically communist or socialist factors (Soviet influence, Marxist-Leninist doctrine, Party dominance of institutions, WTO and CEMA membership, and so on), as against the effects of factors that we might reasonably expect to shape foreign policies within any group of states linked by history, geography, shared values, or economic transactions.

But to return to the immediate purposes of this volume and the approach adopted by the authors. We fully agree with the views expressed by Horelick that comparison is useful only if it combines empirical research with theoretical inquiry. More specifically, this means the testing of a number of propositions about foreign policy making in communist countries and giving some answers to the controversial questions outlined at the beginning of this Introduction. All four contributors have done their 'homework' of empirical study, and the generalisations, which are of necessity expressed in a condensed form in this volume, have all been substantiated and argued by them elsewhere in more detail.[38]

The volume addresses itself both to the serious student (in the broad sense) of international politics as well as to the practitioner. It is primarily for the benefit of the former that extensive references to the literature have been provided in each chapter — including in the Introduction as the reader will have noticed. The empirical content of the chapters may be of interest to both. But what about the theoretical considerations? The practitioner interested in policy related studies may well ask the same question as a thoroughly disgusted senior scholar at the end of an exhaustive (and inconclusive) discussion of the advantages and disadvantages of the application of the bureaucratic politics model to the study of Soviet foreign policy, namely, 'Why do we need models?' It could be asked, 'Why do we need theory?' Three examples may serve to show why the consideration of models, theories, or conceptual frameworks is not a boring and sterile scholastic endeavour but a serious matter with potentially significant practical consequences.

Firstly, there is good reason to argue that the equation of Soviet and Chinese communism with fascism under the conceptual heading of 'totalitarianism', with 'external aggression' being one of the primary manifestations, has tended to obscure the fact that Soviet and Chinese foreign policy *can* be differentiated, flexible and open to compromise. Secondly, the conceptual lenses through which 'monolithism' and 'international communism' appeared as one unified phenomenon in the 1950s and early 1960s blurred the extent to which the USSR and China were already at odds with each other on many questions of world politics. It can only be a matter of conjecture whether US policy in South-east Asia in the 1960s would have taken a different turn if American leaders had shown a greater appreciation of the disintegration of a secular faith and the resourcefulness of national communisms. Thirdly, and more to the point in the context of foreign policy making in communist countries even such a seemingly esoteric topic as the bureaucratic politics model is of importance: whether or not internal groups are pursuing interests of their own or, more broadly, whether internal monolithism is as much of a fiction as the previously held image of monolithic international communism, makes a vital difference for the conduct of Western policy. If there is significant differentiation, policy can be conducted to discourage or encourage particular groups and to strengthen or weaken their hands in domestic controversies. Conversely, such a course of action would be meaningless if it could be shown that commonly accepted operational principles, centralisation, the role of the Party and ideology severely limited the scope of internal disagreement in communist countries.

In the presentation of the papers a division of labour has been adopted. Some of the more general problems of organisational setting, the role of ideology and Party-state relations, and their significance for foreign policy making, will be treated more at length in the chapters on the Soviet Union and China. The rationale of this is that the Soviet Union, needless to say, is the country where a Communist Party (so named in 1918 at the VII Party Congress) first came to power and from where the 'Soviet experience' was disseminated, and China the country where the deviation from that experience has gone farthest: comparison of the two countries can best show the extent to which there is a common basis. The chapters on Romania and the GDR are more detailed analyses of a case study type, one major research focus being a sensitive area — economics — where differences in relative autonomy and responsiveness to domestic pressures are most likely to appear. A final word may be in place with regard to the title of this volume. Foreign policy making in 'communist countries' has been selected not because any of the authors wish to make an ideological point or, for that matter, are under the illusion that communism has been or will soon be achieved in any of the countries under discussion, but simply because the Communist Party is an important (some would say the most important) factor in policy making. The idea of selecting foreign policy making in 'socialist countries' was dismissed because it would have given rise to confusion with many countries in Africa and Asia. However, in the text both terms, communist and socialist, have been used, such use meeting requirements of stylistic variety and the author's individual preference.

Notes

[1] To adapt the definition of his subject by George Modelski, *The Commun-*

ist International System (Princeton: Center for International Studies, 1960), p. 45.

[2] See for example Frederic J. Fleron, ed., *Communist Studies and the Social Sciences* (Chicago: Rand-McNally, 1969); Roger E. Kanet, ed., *The Behavioral Revolution and Communist Studies* (New York: Free Press, 1971); R.C. Tucker, 'On the Comparative Study of Communism', *World Politics*, XIX (1967), pp. 242-57; and H.G. Skilling, 'Soviet and Communist Politics: A Comparative Approach', *Journal of Politics*, 22 (1960), pp. 300-13.

[3] See Andrzej Korbonski, 'Bureaucracy and Interest Groups in Communist Societies: The Case of Czechoslovakia', *Studies in Comparative Communism*, 4, 1 (January 1971), pp. 57-79.

[4] For example Daniel N. Nelson, 'Subnational Political Elites in a Communist System: Contrasts and Conflicts in Romania', *East European Quarterly*, X, 4 (Winter 1976), pp. 459-94.

[5] Henry Krisch, 'Politics in the German Democratic Republic', *Studies in Comparative Communism*, IX, 4 (Winter 1976), pp. 389-419. More generally, see Joseph LaPalombara, 'Monoliths or Plural Systems: Through Conceptual Lenses Darkly', *Studies in Comparative Communism*, VIII, 3 (Autumn 1975), pp. 305-32; Patrick O'Brien, 'On the Adequacy of the Concept of Totalitarianism', *Studies in Comparative Communism*, III, 3 (January 1970), pp. 55-60; and Robert Burrowes, 'Totalitarianism: The Revised Standard Version', *World Politics*, XXI, 2 (January 1969), pp. 272-94.

[6] This is a point made by Alfred G. Meyer with regard to the Soviet system in 'The Functions of Ideology in the Soviet Political System', *Soviet Studies*, XVII, 3 (January 1966), p. 273.

[7] This is the valid criticism made by Charles Gati in his introductory remarks to a symposium on the comparative study of communist foreign policies in *Comparative Communism*, VIII, 1-2 (Spring/Summer 1975), pp. 7-9.

[8] Stephen F. Cohen, 'Politics and the Past: The Importance of Being Historical' (Review article), *Soviet Studies*, XXIX, 1 (January 1977), p. 138.

[9] Ibid., pp. 139-40.

[10] William Faulkner on American slavery, as quoted in ibid., p. 140.

[11] A lengthy bibliography could be compiled of monographs, conference papers, articles and books stressing the conflict nature of communist politics. To name but a few early examples: Joel J. Schwartz and William R. Keech, 'Group Influence and the Policy Process in the Soviet Union', *American Political Science Review*, LXII, 3 (September 1968), pp. 840-51 on the 1958 Educational Reform Act; Philip D. Stewart, 'Soviet Interest Groups and the Policy Process', *World Politics*, XXII, 1 (1969), pp. 29-50 on Khrushchev's plans for 'production education' in 1964; and Sidney T. Ploss, *Conflict and Decision-Making in the Soviet Union* (Princeton, N.J.: Princeton University Press, 1965) on agricultural policy under Khrushchev. There are enormous differences as to what actually is the primary source of conflict. Whereas the works cited above tend to see

the problem very much in terms of interest groups, the idea of personal power struggle is being stressed by others — including by some of those who would like to be counted among the members of the 'conflict school' of Kremlinology (see below, next footnote).

[12] We are grateful to Seweryn Bailer for making this point.

[13] The term 'conflict school' was coined by Carl A. Linden in *Khrushchev and the Soviet Leadership* (Baltimore, Md.: The Johns Hopkins Press, 1966). In Linden's view, among those specialists who had adopted a 'broad outlook' of this kind are to be counted Robert Conquest, Robert Tucker, Sidney Ploss, David Burg, Peter Wiles, Boris Meissner, Wolfgang Leonhard and Victor Zorza. If there is merit to this list, Michel Tatu and Robert Slusser should be added to it. Linden makes it clear that he, too, is an adherent of this distinguished camp.

[14] Arnold L. Horelick, A. Ross Johnson and John D. Steinbruner, *The Study of Soviet Foreign Policy: Decision-Theory-Related Approaches*, Sage Professional Papers: International Studies Series, Vol. 4 (1975), p. 31.

[15] Bogdan Denitch, 'The Domestic Roots of Foreign Policy in Eastern Europe', in Charles Gati, ed., *The International Politics of Eastern Europe* (New York: Praeger, 1976), p. 239.

[16] R. Barry Farrell, 'East European Foreign Policy Leadership, 1964-70', *Studies in Comparative Communism*, IV, 1 (January 1971), pp. 80-96.

[17] Robert Weiner, 'Albanian and Romanian Deviance in the United Nations', *East European Quarterly*, VII, 1 (Spring 1973), pp. 65-90.

[18] For example, Andrzej Korbonski, 'External Influences on Eastern Europe', in Gati, *The International Politics of Eastern Europe*, pp. 253-74.

[19] Robert M. Slusser, *The Berlin Crisis of 1961: Soviet American Relations and the Struggle for Power in the Kremlin, June-November 1961* (Baltimore and London: The Johns Hopkins University Press, 1973).

[20] Herbert S. Dinerstein, *The Making of a Missile Crisis: October 1962* (Baltimore: Johns Hopkins University Press, 1976).

[21] Several such articles have been submitted to *Soviet Studies* (University of Glasgow) but the Editorial Board did not find them acceptable for publication. The names of the authors must remain confidential.

[22] Bernard C. Cohen, 'Foreign Policy', *International Encyclopaedia of the Social Sciences*, Vol. 5 (Macmillan-Free Press, 1968), p. 534. The comments were echoed five years later by Michael Haas, who observed that the field of foreign policy analysis 'has consisted largely of case studies rather than of systematic comparisons across countries'. 'On the Scope and Methods of Foreign Policy Studies', *International Year Book of Foreign Policy Studies*, I (1973), p. 49. But, to make matters worse, the number of useful, thoroughly researched case studies has been extremely limited.

[23] Ib Faurby, 'The Lack of Cumulation in Foreign Policy Studies: The Case of Britain and the European Community', *European Journal of Political Rese-*

arch, 4 (1976), pp. 205-25.

[24] See for example the comments by Michael Banks, 'The Foreign Policy of the United States', in F.S. Northedge, ed., *The Foreign Policies of the Powers* (London, 1968), p. 40.

[25] R. Naroll and F. Naroll, 'On Bias of Exotic Data', *Man*, 25 (1963), pp. 24-6, cited by Eugene J. Webb et al., *Unobtrusive Measures: Nonreactive Research in the Social Sciences* (Chicago: Rand McNally, 1970), p. 114.

[26] For an early criticism, see Daniel Bell, 'Ten Theories in Search of Reality: The Prediction of Soviet Behavior', *World Politics*, X (April 1958), pp. 327-65; and the comments by T.V. Sathyamurthy, 'From Containment to Interdependence', *World Politics*, XX, 1 (October 1967), pp. 142-3. On China, see Robert Boardman, 'Themes and Explanation in Sinology', in Roger L. Dial, ed., *Advancing and Contending Approaches to the Study of Chinese Foreign Policy* (Halifax, N.S.: Centre for Foreign Policy Studies, Dalhousie University, 1974), pp. 5-50.

[27] See for example the Index of Conformity to Soviet Policy used to study the period 1956-68 by William R. Kintner and Wolfgang Klaiber, *Eastern Europe and European Security* (New York: Dunellen, 1971), pp. 225ff. Similar observations made on more traditional grounds are of course more common.

[28] See Zbigniew Brzezinski, *The Soviet Bloc: Unity and Conflict*, rev. ed. (New York: Frederick A. Praeger, Publishers, 1961); Tadeusz N. Cieplak, 'Some Distinctive Characteristics of the Communist System in the Polish People's Republic', *The Polish review*, XIX, 1 (1974), pp. 52-3; and Adam Bromke, *Poland's Politics* (Cambridge: Harvard University Press, 1967), pp. 127 ff.

[29] For detail on these problems see the contribution by Jeanne Kirk Laux in the present volume.

[30] See, for example, the discussions by Zvi Gitelman, 'Toward a Comparative Foreign Policy of Eastern Europe', in Peter J. Potichnyj and Jane P. Shapiro, ed., *From the Cold War to Detente* (New York: Praeger, 1976), p. 151; and Lawrence Whetten, *Germany's Ostpolitik: Relations between the Federal Republic and the Warsaw Pact Countries* (London: Oxford University Press, 1971), pp. 120-2.

[31] Edwina Moreton, 'The Impact of Detente on Relations Between the Member States of the Warsaw Pact: Efforts to Resolve the German Problem and Their Implications for East Germany's Role in Eastern Europe, 1967-72' (Unpublished Ph.D. dissertation, University of Glasgow, 1977); see also Gerhard Wettig, *Community and Conflict in the Socialist Camp: The Soviet Union, East Germany and the German Question, 1965-1972* (London: C. Hurst, 1975). For further analysis of Soviet-East German differences see also the contribution by Peter Marsh in the present volume.

[32] B. Berelson and G.A. Steiner, *Human Behavior: An Inventory of Scientific Findings* (New York: Harcourt, Brace, World, 1964), p. 12. The criticisms, it should be added, are part of a lengthier defence.

13

[33] Arnold L. Horelick, 'Does the Comparative Approach Merit High Priority?', *Comparative Communism*, VIII, 1-2 (Spring/Summer 1975), p. 40.

[34] Alvin Z. Rubinstein, 'Comparison or Confusion?', ibid., p. 43.

[35] Horelick, 'Does the Comparative Approach Merit High Priority?', p. 41.

[36] 'Imputism' is a term coined by Roy C. Macridis, 'Comparative Politics and the Study of Government: The Search for a Focus', *Comparative Politics*, I, 1 (October 1968), pp. 79-90.

[37] The figures according to Department of State, *The Planetary Product in 1975,* Special Report, No. 33 (May 1977).

[38] Hannes Adomeit, 'Soviet Risk Taking and Crisis Behavior: A Theoretical and Empirical Analysis ', Unpublished PhD dissertation, Columbia University, 1977, which contains two detailed case studies of Soviet behaviour in international crises (Berlin 1948 and 1961), as well as reference to Soviet behaviour in other crises; it is a much extended argument of the policy-oriented paper published prior to that, *Soviet Risk-taking and Crisis Behaviour: From Confrontation to Coexistence?*, Adelphi Paper, No. 101 (London: IISS, 1973). Jeanne Kirk Laux, 'Intra-Alliance Politics and European Détente: The Case of Poland and Rumania', *Comparative Communism*, VIII, 1-1 (Spring/Summer 1975), pp. 98-122 and other research on East European countries, notably Romania, published in *Etudes internationales*, IV, 1-1 (mars-juin 1973) and *Journal of Peace Research*, No. 2 (1972). Peter Marsh, 'The Politics of Economic Integration in Eastern Europe with Special Reference to East Germany', M.A. thesis, Manchester University, 1973. Robert Boardman, *Britain and the People's Republic of China, 1949-1974* (London: Macmillan, 1976), and 'Themes and Explanation in Sinology', op. cit.

2 Soviet foreign policy making: the internal mechanism of global commitment

HANNES ADOMEIT

Some of the most striking features of developments in the Soviet Union in the past fourteen years have been the internationally unparalleled stability of the Soviet leadership, the almost complete absence of institutional change (and in some instances the undoing of institutional changes made by Khrushchev), the constant reiteration of standard ideological formulas, declining economic growth rates, and falling productivity.[1] Yet, at first sight paradoxically, the USSR in the same period has embarked on a vigorous armament programme, improving its traditional superiority over NATO forces in the conventional sphere in Central Europe, rising to parity with the USA in the strategic sphere, and acquiring naval and airlift capabilities to intervene, or support intervention, in distant areas (e.g. Angola or Ethiopia). It has also, since 1969, conducted a flexible policy under the slogans of 'peaceful coexistance', 'relaxation of tensions' and 'making the process of détente irreversible'.

According to Lenin (and essentially he was right on that point), 'There is no more erroneous or harmful idea than the separation of foreign from internal policy'.[2] But, as follows from the above enumeration of contradictory elements, the *character* of Soviet foreign policy is different from that of Soviet domestic politics. The provincialism and narrow-minded vindictiveness against dissent and reformism at home stands in stark contrast to the Soviet Union's profile as a global power with commitments ranging from Cuba to Vietnam, world-wide diplomatic representation and Party contacts, scientific activities from pole to pole and in space, far-flung fishing operations (including fishing for intelligence), and considerable and expanding commercial operations. This curious contradiction needs explanation. More specifically, it is appropriate to ask what sort of mechanism of policy making it is that is transforming domestic retrenchment into external activity.

There are a number of broad possibilities which could serve as guidelines to answer that question. Firstly, it could be argued that the apparent difference in the character of Soviet domestic and foreign policy reflects loss of ideological momentum domestically but continuation of such momentum internationally. Secondly, as a stronger variation of this theme, it is conceivable — contrary to the point made above by reference to Lenin — that there *is* a strict separation of the domestic and foreign policy spheres, each one following its own logic and dynamics. (To make the point clear here and now, there is not much evidence for this.) Thirdly, external dynamism could be interpreted as a compensation of sorts for internal weaknesses, a process whereby international glory serves to divert attention from domestic drabness and latent discontent. (If so, there would be parallels to 19th century European imperialism which, too, showed a marked tendency to neglect social, economic and political reform but emphasised the glory of empire building abroad.) To that extent the dichotomy is perhaps more apparent than real: in both spheres of activity, domestic politics and foreign policy, it would be the primary rationale of policy to maintain and expand power. Seen from these perspectives Soviet foreign policy appears as the logical extension of, rather than a puzzling contradiction to, domestic politics.

Evidently, none of these broad possible explanations provides any indication as to whether there exist pressures — and individuals, groups or institutions embodying these pressures — which may be at odds with the present conduct of foreign or domestic policy, or both. They also do not furnish an answer to the question of whether such individuals, groups or institutions adopt congruent attitudes on issues of domestic (including economic), intra-bloc and foreign policy, and policy within the international communist movement.[3]

To put analysis of these problems in some kind of order it is appropriate to begin by looking at some of the broad, long term factors of Soviet policy making, including ideology, power and the bureaucracy. Based on the discussion of bureaucracy an attempt will be made to illuminate in some detail the interests and probably influence of some of the bureaucracies. Considering the rise of the Soviet Union to military-strategic parity with the USA, the revised Western estimates of Soviet defence expenditures as being between 11 and 13 per cent of GNP, estimates that almost as much as 50 per cent of the total output of machinery goes to military 'needs', the fact that Soviet military aid to developing countries exceeds economic aid by a factor of ten, it is appropriate to focus in some detail on the role of the military in foreign policy making. As economic and military problems are closely linked, and as it is possible to see the Soviet emphasis on heavy industry and military power as the result of a series of defeats for such interest groups or bureaucracies promoting economic goals, it is necessary to look also at the likely foreign policy interests and attitudes of economic administrators, 'technocrats', managers and the 'agricultural lobby'. This leads to a criticism of attempts to tie military, economic, political and ideological factors into one single framework of analysis. The final section deals with the problem of generational change and its possible implication for future foreign policy making.

The 'end of ideology'

Western specialists on Soviet affairs are likely to react to any discussion of the role of Soviet ideology in foreign policy making with expressions of *déjà vu* and boredom, and the comment that there was nothing more to say on a problem that had been discussed *ad infinitum* and 'solved'.[4] The solution of the problem, as touched upon in the introductory essay, presents itself in the form of wide agreement with the view that ideology may have explained something of Soviet foreign policy in the early period (i.e. before Stalin came to power) but that there had been a long evolutionary process, as a result of which national or state interests of the USSR had superseded the ideological dimension of Soviet politics.[5] Brest-Litovsk, the proclamation of NEP, entry in the League of Nations, the Hitler-Stalin pact, the XX Party Congress and the Sino-Soviet split are taken as landmarks supposedly demonstrating the increasingly deep contradiction between national and state interests and ideology.

This perceived contradiction is seen as being reinforced by another. 'Ideological' is usually associated with 'irrational', 'reckless' and 'adventurist' but put in sharp contrast to 'pragmatic', 'opportunist' and 'realistic'. As a consequence, ideology as a factor influencing Soviet policy making is being eroded in the mind of the Western analyst when he is faced with instances where Soviet representatives display diplomatic skill, act as shrewd and calculating businessmen or pay much attention to military power as an instrument of furthering state interests.

A subtheme of this perceived contradiction between ideology and pragmatism is the view that the ideological content of foreign policy is equivalent to the degree of Soviet support to world revolution, more specifically, the extent to which the Soviet Union is willing to employ military force on behalf of local Communists in various areas of the world. As a result, ideology in Soviet foreign policy making is being eroded in the perception of the Western analyst when the Soviet leaders apparently close their eyes to the oppression of local Communists while engaging in cooperation with the oppressors at the state level (as in many countries of the Arab world), stand by with folded arms as Marxist regimes are being crushed (as in Chile) or fail to exploit alleged or real advantages for deepening the 'crisis of capitalism' (as in the wake of the oil crisis after 1973).

These two contradictions add up to a third and main contradiction as seen by Western analysts, namely that between (as mentioned in the Introduction) *Rechtfertigungsideologie* and *Antriebsideologie*, the argument being that the Soviet state is indeed an ideology in power but ideology is merely providing legitimacy (*Rechtfertigung*) to action. i.e. can no longer be regarded as a guide to action and furnishing motivation (*Antrieb*). Proof of this thesis is derived from the undoubtedly valid observation that Marxist-Leninist doctrine has served to justify all sorts of policies. At the inter-Party level it has been used to justify projected governments of national union (Italy), adventurous disregard of mathematical majorities (the Portuguese CP in 1975) and hesitation with regard to popular-front tactics (France). At the state level it is being used to legitimise policies of cooperation with the USA but policies of confrontation towards China.

Several reservations with regard to these contradictions are well in place. First of all, if it is true that the Soviet state is an ideology in power it follows that the contradiction between ideological and state, or national, interests is more apparent than real. What is at issue is not a matter of nationalism supplanting ideology but supplementing it.[6] The reconciliation of apparent contradictions was provided long ago by Stalin in his dictum that 'An internationalist is ready to defend the USSR without reservation, without wavering, unconditionally'.[7] The essence of this doctrinal assertion, of course, is the idea that what serves to enhance Soviet power internationally, simultaneously increases the prospects of world revolution.

From a practical political point of view it would be very comforting if one could accept the idea that such an assertion was nothing but cynicism and pretension out of touch with the reality of world politics. It is not wise to adopt such a view. Dynamic interrelationships between Soviet support for revolutionary transformations abroad, the occasional success of such transformations, and benefits for Soviet power and foreign policy do remain. Cuba is perhaps the best example of such interrelationships. Castro's turn from a brand of liberalism to Marxism-Leninism almost provided the USSR with an extensive strategic-nuclear benefit in 1962 (if Khrushchev's idea of a *fait accompli* had worked out as he had anticipated it would); in the latter half of the 1970s it was Cuban troops who put the Marxist-Leninist MPLA into power in Angola and pulled the chestnuts out of the fire for Mengistu's regime in Ethiopia. Soviet policy making, one suspects, is still deeply affected by the idea that revolutionary transformations first and foremost are a blow to imperialist influence and control - in Cuba and potentially elsewhere in Latin America, in Vietnam and perhaps elsewhere in South-east Asia, in Angola and in other African countries, in Portugal and probably also in France and Italy. Not every revolutionary or pseudo-revolutionary transformation *per se* can be regarded as strengthening the power of the Soviet state, and not in all cases is it possible to say that a Western loss is automatically a Soviet gain. This is the 'objective' state of affairs. Yet it appears that the Soviet leadership is untiring in its optimism that if the correlation is not direct and immediate it will ultimately turn out to be so.

As for the contradiction between ideology and pragmatism, careful distinctions need to be made. To speak of Soviet ideology is to speak of Leninism which is largely an adaptation of Marxism to the Russian social, economic and political setting, providing a set of policy prescriptions and advice on tactics. Such advice can be summed up in the firm belief that the ends justify the means and that manoeuvering, flexibility, pragmatism and opportunism are necessary attributes of policies at home and abroad. To that extent, opportunism or pragmatism can be a reflection of ideologically conscious policy rather than a contradiction to it. As the editor of *Izvestiya* put it 70 years ago at a time of undoubted relevance of ideology for policy making, 'We are convinced that the most consistent socialist policy can be reconciled with the sternest realism and most level-headed practicality'.[8]

But there is one problem. To engage in a series of tactical adjustments under the heading of 'stern realism' in the long run could make policy devoid of any significant ideological content. This could be regarded almost as conforming to the Marxist idea of quantity giving way to qualitative change. It is difficult to say to what extent this has already happened.

To turn to the argument that ideology is merely *ex post facto* justification rather than motivation of policy, on this point too it is useful to express reservations because the distinction looks neat in theory but is not very persuasive in practice. This is perhaps best shown by an analogy. For a tribal medicine man the sacred myths and rituals involving the healing power of snake skins, goat blood and monkey tails are undoubtedly a source of legitimacy for the power he exerts. This is so irrespective of whether he is a complete cynic. Nevertheless, the myths, rituals and taboos can assume important motivating functions under two conditions. The first one is a belief on the part of the medicine man that his power will be improved if he can spread the myths to other tribes. The second is the appearance of internal or external critics who dare call the assumed healing powers of myths and medicine men a deplorable hoax and/or deliberate deception; this is likely to call forth vigorous counteraction.

Both of these conditions seem to exist in Soviet foreign policy. Concerning the first condition there are the hopes connected with spreading Marxism-Leninism to the national-liberation movements of the Third World. Concerning the second condition, the activity of dissidents at home, the Sino-Soviet split, the challenge of 'Eurocommunism', the emphasis of the Carter administration on human rights and the provisions of 'basket 3' of the Helsinki Final Act all point in the same direction, namely that the Soviet leadership *nolens volens* cannot relegate ideology to a place of secondary importance in policy making. To that extent it is possible to summarise that an evolutionary process has taken place. The original ideological fervour (the utopian, revolutionary or missionary aspects of ideology) and the humanistic, emancipatory content of Marxism have given way in the Soviet Union to a greater emphasis on legitimacy. To that extent, there has been a transformation in the functions of ideology. What it does not mean is that ideology no longer matters in foreign policy making.

The ends of power

As with the standard dichotomies between ideology and national interest, and ideology and pragmatism, it is unwise to make a rigid distinction between ideology and power. An effective, persuasive ideology can be an important means of exerting influence, and to that extent constitutes a form of power; conversely, power in its traditional dimension (i.e. military and economic power) can be an effective instrument to spread ideology. This is the general frame of reference.[9] Looking specifically at Soviet foreign policy it is obvious that a shift of emphasis has taken place.

In the pre-World War II era the Soviet political leaders often had to make a virtue of necessity, namely to attempt to expand influence with the help of local Communist Parties without being able to come to their aid. In fact, due to the vulnerability of the Soviet state precisely the opposite was the rule: the local Parties had to come to the aid of the Soviet

20

/

Union, the most noteworthy examples being the popular front tactics of the 1930s and the support required of the various Communist Parties for the Hitler-Stalin pact. The Second World War dramatically altered this state of affairs. Military power, either in the form of direct involvement, deterrence or threat, or in the form of weapons deliveries, could be and was used to further Soviet state interests, as well as in attempts to achieve and safeguard 'revolutionary transformations' abroad, first in Eastern Europe, later in the Middle East, Congo, Laos, Cuba and Vietnam and, most recently, in a number of countries in Africa.

Although this use of military power in direct or indirect form is not an unambiguous success story, and does not necessarily add up to a direct correlation between growth in power and growth in political influence, it is fair to say that the Soviet leaders believe that, roughly, there is such a correlation. So far, they have had no negative experiences with military strength (only with military weakness), and so far there has been no traumatic lesson taught to them as it was to the Germans and the Japanese in World War II, and the Americans in Vietnam. Despite significant weaknesses in economics, the ascendancy of the USSR to military-strategic parity has made it possible for the Soviet leaders to come closer to their goal of political equality with the United States. Domestically, the armed forces remain an important instrument in the building of 'socialist man'.

All these factors reinforce each other to warrant the conclusions that: (1) the Soviet leaders are now concerned less with dangers to Soviet security than with opportunities of extending influence; (2) military power is high on the list of their priorities — an observation that will be of relevance later in the context of the role of the military in policy making.

Endless bureaucracy

In addition to ideology and power, Soviet policy making proceeds in the context of a third factor of major importance: the bureaucracy. Despite, as Soviet political leaders and commentators repeatedly put it, the on-going 'scientific-technological revolution' (NTR: *nauchno-tekhnicheskaya revolyutsiya*) and the complex demands it creates, Soviet politics, society and economics remain overshadowed by the Tsarist past, not only as regards the tradition of absolutism and autocracy but also the bureaucratic tradition, including rigid adherence to administrative routine, red tape, procrastination, intriguing, scheming and infighting, and a general indifference to the plight of the individual. The Stalinist period did much to resurrect the all-pervasive power of the bureaucracy. To Trotsky socialism in the Soviet Union suffered a profound bureaucratic degeneration, the bureaucrats having become the single most powerful element in society.

Drawing on Max Weber's theory of bureaucracy, many Western analysts agree largely with this kind of characterisation. For Alfred Meyer the Soviet Union is one 'large complex bureaucracy', the whole society 'a bureaucratic command structure, with all of the features familiar to students of bureaucracy'.[10] 'In all industrialised countries much of the politics that counts is bureaucratic politics', writes T.H. Rigby, but in his view this is

> overwhelmingly the case in the Soviet Union. By the character of their reports and advice, by the twist they give to policies and decrees in putting them into practice, by their departmental style and 'culture', by their successes in struggles over jurisdiction and reorganisation, by their use of personnel powers to reward friends and punish enemies, by the effectiveness of their informal communication and patronage links, by their access to top leadership, Soviet party and government officials participate crucially in the determination of political outcomes.[11]

Several reasons have been advanced for the existence of such a state of affairs. Some of them are the 'far wider scope of government' in the USSR as compared to Western political systems, 'the limited character of the public political process'[12] and the system of *nomenklatura* (central allocation of important posts in the hierarchies of state and Party). The point of all this is that

> in the USSR, despite distinctions between party, government, social organisations, etc., there is an important sense in which all are part of one great single hierarchy. . . . It is as if the Establishment division of the British Treasury guided or approved all appointments, from the editorship of a provincial newspaper or a trade union secretaryship in Scotland up to a ministerial appointment and down to a managerial post in the Midlands.[13]

As argued by Astrid von Borcke, it is also important to note in this context that the Soviet political system officially still aims at asserting the primacy of politics over society and that it attempts to treat the whole of social life as one unified organisation.[14] As Brezhnev has emphasised, 'Every diminution of the leading role of the Party jeopardises the achievements of socialism'.[15] Although the Party's claim that it is expressing a 'scientifically founded' common interest excludes public policy in the sense of competition of ideas, leaders and interests, the exclusion of social, economic and political groups, except for those sanctioned and controlled by the Party, has the result of allocating to the bureaucracy an important integrative function in the body politic. (This, too, was noticed by Trotsky. He argued that the means of production belonged to the state. 'However, the state belongs to the bureaucracy.') Hence, if the Soviet system is one of the most bureaucratised in the modern world, this is so not only because bureaucracy is implementing policy but also and mainly because it is exclusively the various bureaucracies which are authorised to participate in the decision making process.

This type of bureaucratisation shows features *sui generis* which so far have not sufficiently been recognised conceptually. It is a politicised bureaucracy. Its main loyalty does not belong to any particular office or concrete purpose, in accordance with the Weberian concept of 'rational rule', but to the Party — a phenomenon expressed in the term *partiinost'*. Hence, the authority of an official depends less on the office itself but on the degree of political protection he receives; the main criterion for his appointment or advancement is political reliability; and 'the advancement and protection of sectional interests and commitments depends mainly on the behind-the-scenes efforts of sympathetic officials'.[16] The essence of politics in the Soviet Union, therefore, can be regarded as lying in the interaction between powerful leaders, their adherents and the organisations over which they preside.[17]

Many of the basic problems, goals and interests of the regime find their expression in the positions and the interaction of the big bureaucracies. While it is true that the regime has been able to counteract the tendencies towards autonomy inherent in all bureaucracies — because of the role of the Party, the system of *nomenklatura* and a number of specific features, such as informal relations as in cliques and family circles — it is also valid to assume that each big organistion is in partial conflict with every other; and although all the bureaucracies do have basic goals in common, foremost among which the safeguarding of the regime, they do form nevertheless only a 'coalition' of sorts (Michael Ellman). Political struggle does not proceed in the form of electoral contests. As politics cannot be abolished, this is the very reason why administrative processes are affected by it to such a significant extent. The result produced is that of a form of 'crypto-politics' (T.H. Rigby).[18]

But just as with ideology and power there have been important changes that have affected Soviet bureaucracy. In the early stages of industrialisation it was possible to concentrate efforts on a few tasks of major importance. Coercion and genuine pioneering spirit combined to produce impressive rates of growth in industry. Indeed, in the initial stages of development, centralisation and the command economy made good sense — despite the absence of computer technology. However, as most Western and some East European economists argue, modern industrial society requires a higher degree of specialisation and diversification of functions than in the past; it creates dynamics of its own that can neither be anticipated in detail nor entirely be regulated from above. In such a state of affairs terror becomes counterproductive. A premium is put on voluntary cooperation and initiative at lower levels of decision making.

The result of this development for the purpose of the present inquiry is to say that tendentially modern industrial society increases autonomy of the individual bureaucracies and potentially enhances their role in foreign policy making. More detailed consideration of this problem will show whether these tendencies and potentialities have found their reflection in the actual state of affairs in the Soviet Union,.

There are some affinities in conceptual approach between the consideration of bureaucracy and bureaucracies, and the focus on interest groups in the study of policy making in the USSR. According to Gordon Skilling's introduction to the anthology *Interest Groups in Soviet Politics:*

> There can be no doubt that communist society, in spite of its monolithic appearance and the claims of homogeneity made by its supporters, is in fact as complex and stratified as any other, and is divided into social classes. . . . Each group has its own values and interests, and each its sharp internal differences, and all are inescapably involved in conflict with other groups.[19]

Skilling's central assumption, that the Soviet political system passed through a period of transition and had arrived at a stage characterised by an increased activity of political interest groups, is shared by many other Western analysts, by Jerry Hough, for instance, who expressed these images in the term 'institutional pluralism' of Soviet society and politics,[20] and by Milton Lodge who traced élite-group attitudes in a content analysis of Soviet periodicals.[21] What, then, are those 'interest groups' in the Soviet setting?

Judging from the table of contents of the anthology by Skilling and Griffiths, Soviet interest groups include the Party *apparatchiki*, the security police, the military, the industrial managers, the economists, the writers and the jurists. In this list one might also want to include the specialists of international affairs at the various institutes of the USSR Academy of Sciences and the Foreign Ministry's Institute of International Relations (IMO), a category which has been called the *institutchiki* (Arnold Horelick). As this enumeration shows there will be a great deal of overlap between the two approaches because all of the important interest groups are at the same time officially sanctioned bureaucracies. On this basis the following argument has been developed by Western observers: the interests represented by the leaders of the various groups are primarily functional interests; attitudes and the direction of influence exerted can be inferred, or predicted, from the axiom of 'Where you stand depends on where you sit'.[22]

But this is precisely where major problems arise: Is it really safe to assume that the leaders on top of the various bureaucracies are primarily functional representatives of the various bureaucracies, or are they representatives of the Politburo in the bureaucracies? Assuming that the former is largely true, what exactly are the interests of the various bureaucracies in foreign policy? (So far, most of the Western discussion has been limited to examining the role of the various bureaucracies and interest groups in domestic politics.) Assuming that one can arrive at a reasonably accurate reconstruction of interests, the problem that arises next is to see whether attempts are being made by the interest groups / bureaucracies to exert influence on foreign policy making in a direction corresponding with their interests and attitudes. Finally, if such attempts are being made, it would be interesting to see whether they are effective for all types of decision, e.g. decisions concerning day-to-day business, decisions of principle and far-reaching consequence, and decisions in international crises. These are complex questions which cannot be answered within the limited scope of this article (if at all). But it is useful at this stage to abandon the broad framework of ideology, power and bureaucracy — which could be compared to the horizontal bar of a 'T' — and probe more deeply, along the vertical bar of the 'T', into the roles played by specific institutions, bureaucracies or groups.

The role of the military

Analysis of interests and attitudes of the Soviet military and Party military relations has been shaped significantly by the writings of Roman

25

Kolkowicz, by his view that there existed some kind of adversary relationship between the Soviet military and the Party, the military stressing professional autonomy, nationalism, detachment from society, heroic symbolism and élitist organisational goals, the Party emphasising ideological orthodoxy, proletarian internationalism, social involvement, anonymity and egalitarian ideals.[23] This theme is taken up by Kolkowicz in his contribution to Skilling and Griffith's anthology where he argues that the military's relations with the Party are characterised by instability, but that there had been 'noticeable success in the efforts of the military to obtain institutional autonomy'.[24] As an extension of this argument, it seemed to many observers at the time that the appointment of Marshal Grechko to full membership in the Politburo in April 1973 was a manifestation of this very trend of allegedly greater institutional autonomy and increased influence of the military in policy making.

However, this line of reasoning, stressing the conflicting nature of Party military relations and the growing influence of the Soviet military is too simplistic, and perhaps even misleading. Military-patriotic education, discipline, devotion to duty, conservatism, and ideological orthodoxy are preferences which are shared by the military as well as by the Party *apparatchiki*. To assume a discrepancy between the current interpretations of proletarian internationalism and nationalism is problematic in itself, but to divide these principles in terms of Party military conflict is even more problematic. Assumptions that the military is always the advocate of a high degree of professionalism, innovation and technical expertise evade the question of whether it is not precisely the Party that utilises the central *apparat* to give new ideas and military science a push and introduce them into the armed forces, often against conservative and traditional elements in the military. This would be true in particular for foundation of the Strategic Rocket Forces under Khrushchev. But it would be even more correct with regard to the Soviet Navy, traditionally weak a branch of the armed forces at a disadvantage *vis-a-vis* the other branches: it is hardly conceivable that the expansion of its role could have been achieved without the active support of the political leadership (and, most likely, against resistance by other branches).[26]

In the light of these arguments, it would appear that the consistent practice of appointing military professionals to the post of Defence Minister and Grechko's inclusion in the Politburo were not the harbingers of 'Bonapartism' or a rise to power of the military at the expense of the Party, not indications of greater institutional autonomy of the military, but manifestations of a deliberate policy by the Party to ensure effectiveness of control and speedy implementation of politico-military decisions taken at the level of the Politburo or the Defence Council.[27] Similarly, Ustinov's appointment to the post of Defence Minister in April 1976 should not be taken as a reversal of the respective fortunes of the Party and the military (i.e. as a victory of the Party over the military) and the ascendancy of civilian over military priorities; it is more likely the result of a number of things, partly a reward for long services rendered, partly a response to the necessity of coordinating increasingly complex decisions in defence economics, and hence partly an indication of the Soviet leadership's awareness of interrelationships between an efficient economic and scientific-technological base and effective military power.[28]

But what about those instances where the Soviet military played a role in domestic power struggles? It is fair to argue that where it did play a role it did so not in the form of pushing itself into the political limelight to further its own power ambitions as a politicised institution and at the expense of the Party but because it was invited in, for a limited time span, by the political leadership or a major faction of it. This applies to all the three major instances that are relevant in this context: the arrest and execution of Beria and the curtailment of the power of the secret police in 1953-54; the help the military gave Khrushchev in 'reversing a mathematical majority' in the Presidium in June 1957; and the support it extended to the Presidium in removing Khrushchev from office in October 1964.

A fourth example often cited to underline the conflicting nature of the relationship between the military and the Party is the dramatic ouster of Marshal Zhukov from his posts of Defence Minister and full membership of the Presidium in October 1957 by a plenum of the Central Committee, and the nature of the charges subsequently levelled against him.[29] However, a convincing reconsideration of the Zhukov affair shows that it was primarily an episode 'occasioned by the actions of one man under particular circumstances'; it was undoubtedly a conflict between Zhukov and Khrushchev; and this conflict was inflated by the 'atmosphere of Soviet élite politics'. But it was

> hazardous indeed to assume that the clash between the two was a manifestation of some more profound conflict between the institutions of which they were formal heads. Conflicts do perhaps 'rage in the Kremlin', but the combatants are not necessarily surrogates for larger social structures.[30]

There is another conclusion that emerged from the analysis of the Zhukov affair.

A revised understanding should spur reconsideration of the dichotomous way in which Soviet military politics has been interpreted in the West, in terms of an image of Army and Party locked in implacable conflict and able to agree only on temporary truces. On the contrary, elements of consensus are often as important in this relationship as elements of conflict.[31]

This is not to say that there is a complete absence of conflict over politico-military affairs in the USSR. Yet the nature of conflict is less likely to be dominated by such esoteric concepts as 'professionalism', 'elitism', or 'social involvement' than by highly practical questions, such as budgetary allocations for the various branches of the armed forces, the size of the ground forces, the role and functions of the Soviet Navy, the technical and political implications of armed forces reductions in Central Europe, and the limitation of strategic arms. Also, when conflict does occur it is unlikely to divide the major protagonists into two well-defined camps (i.e. the military versus the Party) but it will produce opinions and attitudes cutting across institutional lines.

It is on the basis of these considerations that the question of the role and influence of the Soviet military in foreign policy could most appropriately be analysed. Kolkowicz writes that in what 'may be described as generic to all military establishments', one of the 'functional interests' of the Soviet military is the 'maintenance of a certain level of international political tension in order to provide the rationale for large military budgets and allocations'.[32] While this may be correct, it tells us nothing about attempts by the military to exert influence on Soviet foreign policy, about effectiveness of these attempts when they are made, or about the problem whether hard line attitudes imply support of the military for ventures which require the acceptance of military risks, as in Berlin in 1961 or in Cuba in 1962, or whether they work for or against military commitments as, let us say, in the Middle East, Angola or Ethiopia.

This last point is of particular importance. Surely, no elaborate quantitative content analysis is needed to prove the obvious, namely that military newspapers and journals, almost everywhere, will have a tendency to stress military aspects of international relations and exaggerate threats to security, real or imagined. As for the Soviet Union, the columns of *Krasnaya zvezda* and *Kommunist vooruzhennykh sil* will obviously tend to emphasise themes such as the incurable aggressiveness of American imperialism and, at least every once in a while, the undiminished possibility of victory in the nuclear age. But to conclude from this that the Soviet military is prone to adventurism and exerts a role to that effect in foreign policy making would be hazardous.

Firstly, it is necessary to question the way in which the attitudes of the military are usually established. The procedure adopted is typically to compare the content of military newspapers and journals, e.g. *Krasnaya zvezda* and *Kommunist vooruzhennykh sil*, with non-military journals, say, *Pravda*, which leads to the (foregone) conclusion that the military has different attitudes and hence advocates different policies from those of the Party. The problem with this procedure lies in the fact that, although the masthead of *Krasnaya zvezda* — the main newspaper of the Soviet armed forces — tells the reader that it is an 'organ of the Ministry of Defence', the newspaper is actually edited under the auspices of the Main Political Administration (MPA) of the Army and Navy, i.e. by an organ of the Party! The bi-weekly journal *Kommunist vooruzhennykh sil* is also edited by the MPA. It follows from this that if military attitudes are, in fact, established in the way as outlined one would most likely be retracing the political line handed down from the Party to the armed forces rather than establish genuine military opinion. Seen from these perspectives, it is not at all surprising to read, in a study of the Soviet military and Soviet policy in the Middle East in 1970-73 as reflected in various Soviet military periodicals, that 'Each of the organs under investigation presented a uniform and consistent line' and that '*Kommunist vooruzhennykh sil* aligns itself consistently and unequivocally with the forward line of *Krasnaya zvezda*'.[33]

A related pitfall is the selection of views expressed by particular officers without regard to their career background and institutional attachment. This is true in particular for inferences frequently drawn in the West from statements of such notorious hardliners as Colonels Rybkin and Bondarenko. Both of them are not professional officers but political officers attached to the MPA. For opinion of the military, or sections or branches thereof, it is necessary to turn to the writings of professional officers. But some caution is advised even then because such writings may be commissioned or even provided by Party organs. Such practice is not uncommon in the Warsaw Pact countries.

A final pitfall rests in the tendency of Western analysts to establish a direct causal relationship between the hard-line, forward oriented 'attitudes' of the military, as expressed in military periodicals, and a successful role of the military in foreign policy making. The above quoted analyst of Soviet policies in the Middle East, 1970-73, consequently summarises that one could infer from the evidence the 'evolving importance of the military as a political pressure group' because of the fact 'that in all the cases (of changes in Soviet policy in the Middle East) referred to in the foregoing analysis the military's "advice" was ... heeded and followed'.[34]

It is at this point that one comes up against the same analytical problem in foreign policy as in Soviet domestic politics, that is, to distinguish between preferences of the military and the political leadership. Soviet political leaders have gone out of their way to stress that, détente notwithstanding, there remains not only a certain level of international political tension, but a 'fundamental contradiction between imperialism and socialism in the world arena' and hence the necessity for vigilance, military preparedness and military budgets. Détente has been explained by the *institutchiki*, the political leadership and, of course, by the military as the direct result of significant changes in the correlation of forces in favour of socialism, i.e. primarily by the growth of Soviet military power.

What this means for the analysis of foreign policy making in the Soviet Union is pointed out clearly by Malcolm Mackintosh who concludes on the basis of three case studies (the Middle East crisis of 1967, the invasion of Czechoslovakia in 1968, and SALT) that 'when a foreign policy adopted by the leadership coincides with military views, it is difficult to distinguish whether the policy was initiated by the Party or by the military'; that in cases where the views of the armed forces might differ from those of the Party leaders, 'there is nothing to suggest any diminution of the Party's ultimate primacy in foreign policy decision making'.[35]

Also, Mackintosh's case studies, this author's own case studies (Berlin 1948, the Middle East 1956 and Berlin 1961), as well as impressions gained from looking at other cases (e.g. Cuba 1962), only serve to underline the point that far from advocating risky and adventurous schemes abroad the Soviet military is tendentially an advocate of caution, taking a conservative approach to the commitment of Soviet military forces outside the immediate Soviet-bloc area.[36] If this is correct the hard-line, forward-oriented themes struck in the military periodicals, and as expressed in the speeches of the Soviet military leaders, appear to have a variety of purposes. They can be devices, as mentioned above by reference to Kolkowicz, to secure and legitimise large allocations for the defence sector. They can serve to support the general ideological theme of the ultimate victory of socialism over capitalism. And they can be a boost to morale in the armed forces because too differentiated or too peaceful a picture of international politics would erode the effectiveness of the leadership's call for vigilance. But taken by themselves they are not indications of a hard line on the substantive issues of East-West confrontations.

It is on the basis of this discussion that preference should be given to the last of the three broad guidelines suggested at the beginning of this chapter for explaining the, on the surface, puzzling contradiction between domestic retrenchment and external activity. The display, maintenance and expansion of power, both at home and abroad, finds two strong advocates in the Soviet political system — the Party and the military. Both of these powerful groups of bureaucracies evidently hope that the social and economic costs (the suppression of dissent, the obstacles to international tourism and the exchange of ideas, the perennial calls for discipline, the low priority for consumer goods production, etc.) will appear less painful against the background of superpower status and global influence.

The role of economics and economic interest groups

It may be useful to start examination of the role of economics, the economic bureaucracy and economic interest groups in foreign policy making by looking at the conflict of economic versus military priorities and at possible interrelationships between relaxation of political tensions, East-West economic exchanges, SALT and the Soviet military posture. Standard Western assumptions are that influx of modern Western technology, opening of the Soviet society to liberal ideas, reformism, and political and military relaxation of tension (détente and SALT) are all inextricably linked. The groups likely to oppose this package of policies are to be found in the military establishment and the Party apparatus. Those likely to support it supposedly come from the ranks of the state bureaucracy and the agricultural and consumer-industrial 'lobbies'; they will most likely include many economists and other experts; and it is these latter groups that are being supported by Brezhnev.

However, appearances may very well be different from reality. Coherence, i.e. a unified approach, may very well exist but so far its main direction and purpose has not been to create feedbacks between influx of Western technology and domestic economic reform but precisely the opposite: to delay, circumvent or make unnecessary basic reforms in the command economy within the overall goal of strengthening the performance of the Soviet economy and broadening its scientific-technological base. If so, it is quite possible that there is, in addition to the issues mentioned above, consensus of policy between the military establishment and the Party leadership also on the type and scope of East-West economic exchanges and arms control agreements. This would be so on the basis of the following considerations of the military establishment: it is necessary to create a sound economic and scientific-technological foundation for military power. Our GNP being only about half of the American equivalent it is evident that in the past extraordinary efforts were needed to achieve parity. Given the fact of our country's declining economic growth rates on the one hand, but rising expectations of the consumer on the other, it may be very difficult in the future to keep up with an economically more powerful and technologically superior superpower. It is therefore advisable to avoid the uncertainties of an accelerated arms race with the USA and try to slow down the pace of US military-technological innovations. The political leadership should therefore try to conclude agreements which safeguard parity but do not rule out superiority when preconditions for it are laid.[37]

To turn to economic interest groups as the assumed proponents of a policy that seeks to create feedbacks between East-West economic exchanges and domestic economic reform, and between external détente and internal liberalisation, one must first try to identify with some precision the dramatis personae. Six broad categories are relevant in the present considerations: 1 the Politburo and the central Party bureaucracy; 2 the central planning and administrative organs, including Gosplan and the economic ministries; 3 the First Secretaries of the provisional party committees (obkoms); 4 the managers; 5 economists, sociologists and other experts; and 6 collective farmers, workers and consumers.

Clearly, not much political power and influence rests in the last two categories of the enumeration compiled above: the collective farmers, workers and consumers (category six) do not appear in an autonomous organised fashion on the Soviet national political scene. Their interests are assumed, deduced and — perhaps surprisingly — met, although at a painfully slow pace. Economists, sociologists and other experts (category five) generate ideas, some of them progressive and reformist, but their power base is non-existent, their access to central decision making limited and their role in implementation of decisions marginal. Also, it would appear that the overwhelming majority of them is quite satisfied with the professional, material and status rewards that the regime seems quite willing to offer and is therefore not prepared to risk privileges by engaging in dissident activities.

There is broad agreement among Western analysts that there is little enthusiasm for reform among the central planning and administrative organs (the second category) and stiff opposition by the First Secretaries of the *obkoms*, the provincial Party committees (third category) and that it is these two groups which are in a powerful position to delay, distort or misdirect almost any sort of reformist venture. This is so despite the fact that they are often in conflict with each other. The reasons for their lack of reformist enthusiasm are not difficult to reconstruct. The *obkom* First Secretaries — Soviet prefects — play an important 'horizontal' coordinating role in the economy intersecting and often improving the 'vertical' flow of instructions from the ministerial bureaucracies.[38] Because of the cumbersome planning mechanism the *obkom* First Secretaries act as intermediaries and arbiters among the managers. This role, at the local level, as well as the role of the central planning and administrative organs, would be much eroded if the basic features of the reforms of 1965 (still at issue in the 1970s) were to be introduced on a large scale, namely expansion of direct contacts between enterprises, expansion of production associations (*firmy* or *ob"edineniya*), aggregate orders to form the basis of the production plan, reduction of central indicators, establishment of incentive funds for financing capital investments by enterprises, and introduction of new success indicators (sales, profit and profitability). Reform attempts of this kind tend to accentuate what many observers see as a basic conflict between power and efficiency.[39]

The only category that is assumed to benefit from economic reforms, and for this reason to support them is that of the managers (category four). Alexander Yanov, a former Soviet journalist, is a strong advocate of this point of view. Summing up his own experiences he paraphrases a Soviet enterprise director to the effect that the Soviet managers have been accustomed to thinking independently. They want to throw off the shackles of Party control and interference. They would be willing to introduce innovative, fundamentally new modes of work organisation and be 'ready to experiment day and night'. And they believe that given a free reign they could not only reach but even surpass, by a wide margin, world standards of labour productivity.[40]

This may be painting a much too favourable picture of the Soviet manager. Obviously, innovation can only mean uncertainty and disruption, at least initially. Decentralisation of economic decision making can only mean that the enterprise director has to take responsibility for his decisions — something he can often avoid now. It is not surprising, therefore, to read that a limited sample of factory directors interviewed by

Yanov though that the proportion of their colleagues who would actively want to participate in a major reconstruction of the Soviet economy was only between 25-30 per cent![41] This picture is rounded off by taking into account that many of the politically important managers are to be found in the ministries, which — as Yanov argues — are anti-reform. So there is no big conflict.

The views of the Politburo (the first category) are difficult to ascertain but opinions in that body are probably divided. There are indications as to differences between Kosygin and Brezhnev which have diligently been reconstructed by Kremlinological procedure, and the respective positions which these leaders adopt (Kosygin in favour of reform, Brezhnev against it) are typically represented as flowing from the functions they fulfil (Kosygin as chief of the state apparatus, and Brezhnev as head of the Party).[42] It is quite possible that there is truth in this reconstruction of the respective positions adopted by Brezhnev and Kosygin; the problem lies only in the juxtaposition of the differences of view according to functional criteria. Offices of the state (including in the economic hierarchy) and the Party are often interchangeable, and officials at the top often hold jobs in both hierarchies.[43] Examination of the educational and occupational composition of the CPSU membership and of its leading bodies suggests that no sharp distinction can be made between the two groups; and that the relation between economic managers and *apparatchiki*, particularly at the higher levels, may more accurately be seen as one of interpenetration and mutual absorption than conflict.[44]

But to revert to the main problem of analysis here. If it is correct that none of the six groups can be regarded as unambiguously advocating domestic economic and, by extension, political reform, and given the fact that the Soviet Union nevertheless has embarked on a broad spectrum of East-West economic exchanges, it follows that there is no positive correlation between domestic reformism and international economic interdependence; that there is, as mentioned above, probably only a negative correlation — evasion of reform by import of Western technology; and that it is the latter purpose which commands a broad consensus in foreign (economic) policy making.[45] These considerations are of relevance when using 'congruence' as a tool for examining interrelationships between Soviet domestic and foreign policy.

'Congruence' as a framework of analysis

At the basis of the framework is postulated an inner logic that links a revisionist attitude in foreign affairs to revisionism at home and in doctrine, and similarly translates sectarianism, or Stalinism, or conservatism into a totality of interlocking views on both internal and external affairs.[46] In the view of Alexander Dallin, who developed this framework of analysis, there is congruence of elements either of the left (ideology, orthodoxy, internationalism, mobilisation, adventurism, priority of heavy industry and emphasis on vigilance and arms efforts) or the right (pragmatism, reformism, nationalism, gradualism, relaxation of tensions, priority of light industry and emphasis on agriculture and consumer goods production), such congruence simultaneously affecting doctrine and behaviour, domestic, intra-bloc and foreign policy, and policy in the international communist movement.[47]

As for the bureaucracies, institutions or interest groups advocating this or that particular line of policy, there are correspondingly assumed to exist two major benches, on one sitting the exponents of the military-industrial complex (including the military, the supervisors of defence industry and those engaged in heavy industrial production, ideologues and orthodox Party *apparatchiki*, and on the other the members of the agricultural and consumer goods lobby, the economic reformers, the pragmatists and experts. (Vernon Aspaturian speaks of two similarly broad groupings, a 'security-productionist-ideological' coalition and a 'consumptionist-agricultural-public sector' coalition.)[48] These differentiations are applied to current conditions in the following way: 'Soviet pronouncements in 1970-72 suggest a new preponderance of the moderates and their continued alliance with the consumer goods and agricultural lobbies'; speculation is warranted to the effect 'that the advocates of gross strategic parity with the United States have carried the day over those pushing for a serious try to achieve strategic superiority . . .'[49]

There are many problems with this framework of analysis. Firstly, it lends itself to the fostering of simplistic ideas, in particular the notion that Soviet domestic politics and foreign policy inevitably and incurably call forth a fundamental split in the leadership between 'hawks and doves', which, as one Kremlinologist characteristically wrote, manifested itself 'on every major issue' of politics.[50]

Secondly, the dichotomy into left and right may be a useful framework for analysing certain periods in the history of Soviet foreign policy but it is doubtful whether it is of help in the analysis of the present era. Current Soviet domestic, intra-bloc and, more generally, foreign policy, as well as policy of the CPSU within the international communist movement, is characterised by increasing complexity. Simple solutions, if they ever existed, are no longer available. Confrontation with one major power (say China) may require compromises with another (e.g. the United States); a hard line towards one European country (say, West Germany in the period 1966-68) may be accompanied by a soft line towards another (e.g. France, precisely for the reason of bringing pressure to bear on West Germany by virtue of a Franco-Soviet rapprochement); isolation of one Eurocommunist Party leader (Carrillo), may go hand in hand with indifference towards or annoyance with another (Marchais) and friendly relations with a third (Berlinguer).

Thirdly, the framework is incapable of solving contradictions not only when it comes to specific issues of policy but also when one looks at individual Soviet leaders in their assumed role as representatives of functional interests and bureaucracies. For instance, Molotov has correctly been regarded as one of the foremost examples of a 'leftist' in the Soviet context, due to his orthodox Stalinist outlook, his emphasis on priority production of heavy industry, etc., yet at the same time there is convincing evidence that he warned against any leftist adventurism in the Middle East.[51] Khrushchev is being regarded as the prototype of all the elements of the right, yet at the same time his was a most serious and most direct approach to the diplomacy of threat and superpower confrontation. To Suslov has been attributed a consistently left outlook and a hard line on ideological and foreign political matters, ranging from China to the 1961 Berlin crisis, from vigorous encouragement of the national liberation struggles to support for the Portuguese CP's attempt in 1975 to win power through revolutionary means, but at the same time he is being credited with having been strongly opposed to Soviet intervention in Czechoslovakia.[52] Andropov, in his capacity as head of the KGB, is said to have played a major role in the Soviet decision to intervene in Czechoslovakia, and subsequently in the attempts to restore ideological orthodoxy throughout the bloc, yet at the same time he is reported as being a liberal in the Soviet context.[53] Brezhnev poses the ultimate problem for the validity of congruence: for years being regarded as the prototype of the unimaginative, orthodox Party *apparatchik*, as an advocate of close cooperation with the military and the military-industrial complex (due to his association of long standing with both), is now being seen as the chief architect of détente, as the flag bearer of the moderates and the agro-consumer complex. Clearly, something is amiss.

Fourthly, the framework has a tendency to overlook or belittle one of the most typical and basic features of Soviet policy, namely the deliberate balancing of policies of the left by elements of the right so as to main-

36

tain overall coherence of policy. This basic feature can be traced all the way back to Lenin. When in 1921 the New Economic Policy was being promulgated, with all the — from the Bolshevik point of view — possible negative consequences, such as erosion of ideological fervour and the danger of slipping back to capitalism, this was attempted to be held in check by the imposition of increased discipline in the Party by the outlawing of 'factionalism'. Similarly, the present Soviet verbal emphasis on détente, arms control agreements, the authorisation of contacts with the West on selected levels, increase in East-West economic exchanges, and some gestures to assuage Western opinion aroused by the harsh treatment of dissidents, all these elements are accompanied by extensive efforts to impose ideological orthodoxy and discipline in the Soviet bloc. In fact, the beginning of the current Soviet peace offensive (Spring 1969) coincided with a much more severe turning of the screw in Czechoslovakia: only when normalisation had been achieved to relative Soviet satisfaction, and the seeds of reformism in Eastern Europe seemingly been contained, did the USSR embark on détente policies abroad. All this points to basic coherence of policy but not to left-right congruence.

Generational change and its implications for the future

The argument as it has been developed thus far emphasises coherence of policy and consensus about basic principles of foreign policy rather than internal conflict and suggests that distinctions between 'hawks' and 'doves' in the Soviet leadership are blurred. Such differences as may exist in the Politburo are most likely not clear cut or permanent, following primarily functional lines, but variable, depending on the issue of foreign policy, relative power positions and individual preferences. This argument about leadership consensus and policy coherence if comparison is made with other political systems rests on a number of factors. One of them is the similarity of background, age, experience and outlook of the top foreign policy makers. It is appropriate to provide some detail about this problem.

Judging from all (or the little) evidence there is, and from the nature of responsibilities and the status acquired, the following 15 men can be considered the inner core of the foreign policy establishment: Brezhnev, the General Secretary of the Party, Chairman of the Supreme Soviet and Chairman of the Defence Council (*Sovet oborony*); Kosygin, Chairman of the Council of ministers; Suslov, Second Secretary of the Party Central Committee and top foreign policy assistant to Brezhnev among the Central Committee secretaries; Gromyko, Minister of Foreign Affairs; Andropov, Chairman of the KGB (an institution that has the functions of the CIA in addition to those of internal security); D.S. Ustinov, Minister of Defence and Secretary of the CC in charge of defence industry; B.N. Ponomarev, Secretary of the Party Central Committee and head of its International Department; V. Rusakov, Secretary of the Party Central Committee and head of its Socialist Countries Department; I.V. Arkhipov, Deputy Chairman of the Council of Ministers and Chairman of the Council of Ministers' Foreign Economic Commission; N.S. Patolichev, Minister of Foreign Trade; S.A. Skachkov, Chairman of the State Committee for Foreign Economic Relations (despite its title, really the foreign aid agency); N.M. Pegov, head of the Foreign Personnel Department of the Central Committee; A.M. Aleksandrov-Agentov, Personal Assistant to the General Secretary; and G.M. Kornienko and V.F. Mal't-sev, both of them First Deputy Ministers of Foreign Affairs.[54]

As shown by Jerry Hough, the majority of the top decision makers in foreign policy were born between 1904 and 1909 (i.e. most of them are now in their 70's), they came from backgrounds of lower work and/or lower social status but managed to go to college and graduate from specialised technical, engineering or agricultural institutes during or shortly after the period of the First Five-Year Plan period (1928-32) and came to hold important jobs in the Party and state hierarchies after the Purges and during the war. Not only were the top Soviet foreign policy makers, as the jargon does, affected by similar socialisation processes, but they also have worked together for a very extended period of time. In fact, five of the most important officials — Suslov, Gromyko, Ponomarev, Patolichev and Skachkov — have held their present job for at least 20 years. In no other major country have officials been occupying central foreign policy posts for comparable lengths of time. As an illustration of this, and as an indication of the differences between the USA and the USSR in this respect, Hough writes that

> It is mind-boggling to think that the present head of the international department of the Central Committee [Ponomarev] was appointed a key member of the Comintern Executive Committee [in 1936] to help implement the Popular Front when President Carter was 12 years old and Zbigniew Brzezinski was 8, that the present Minister of Foreign Affairs was serving as Ambassador to the United States 7 years later and dealing with President Roosevelt and

[Secretary of State] Cordell Hull and that the major Central Committee secretary for foreign policy [Suslov] was speaking before the Cominform at roughly the time of the Stalin-Tito split [in 1948].[55]

However, much as the current leaders may regret it, neither have the achievements of Soviet gerontology progressed far enough to make them (the Soviet leaders) immortal, nor is it true, as Kirilenko asserted at Brezhnev's birthday celebrations in 1976, that 70 years of life in the Soviet Union is 'considered only middle age'.[56] Generational change is inevitable, and it will take place soon, the question is only, who will be the new leaders, and what policies are they likely to adopt?

Undoubtedly, one of the starting points for well-founded conjectures about future trends in foreign policy making is to emphasise the high degree of professionalisation and specialisation that has taken place in the middle echelons of the foreign policy establishment, both in the Central Committee apparatus responsible for international problems and in the Ministry of Foreign Affairs. Middle-level officials in these two organs, who are now in their late 40's and 50's, are often graduates from MGIMO (Moscow State Institute for International Relations, which is under the auspices of the Ministry of Foreign Affairs) and they have broad experience within their respective institutions and/or in journalism dealing with international problems. A virtual explosion of international relations institutes under the auspices of the Academy of Sciences of the USSR has taken place in the post-Stalin era, and in several instances it is a well established fact that the more important heads of these institutes even now have some role in foreign policy making *vis-à-vis* non-communist countries. This is true in particular for Georgii A. Arbatov (Director of the Institute of the USA and Canada and a candidate member of the CPSU Central Committee) who is said to have close ties to Brezhnev and acts as consultant on US-Soviet relations for the CC apparatus. A similarly important role in the same apparatus can be attributed to Nikolai N. Inozemtsev (formerly First Deputy Chief of *Pravda*, and currently head of the Institute of World Economy and International Relations and a candidate member of the CC). Finally, among the links between specialists and policy makers, one might also want to list Anatoly A. Gromyko, the son of the Soviet Foreign Minister, who is head of the Institute of Africa at the Academy of the USSR and who may contribute some expertise to the Soviet Union's policy towards Africa.[57] The conclusions generally drawn from these processes of professionalisation and specialisation are that the coming generation of foreign policy makers in the Soviet Union will not only be better trained and better informed but also more inclined to rational solution, more amenable to accommodation with the world outside and hence easier to deal with.

While this may be so it is important to balance these trends by observations pointing in the opposite direction. Looking at the pattern of political succession in the USSR (which can be taken here as a more specific form of the broader problem of generational change) it is evident that in the past those in control of the Party levers (e.g. Stalin, Khrushchev and Brezhnev) were in the best position to win power in the succession struggle and fill important posts with their own adherents. It is also noteworthy that those leaders appealing to hard-line, dogmatic, fundamentalist or uncompromising sections of the Soviet power élite, who seemed to have good contacts with and who promised support for the military (Khrushchev in 1953-54 and Brezhnev in 1964-65) succeeded in outmanoeuvering those rivals who (like Khrushchev before his fall) often pursued soft options, or who (like Beria and Malenkov in 1953-55) were trying to map out a new course, attempting to base their support on non-Party organs and appealing to what, as noted above, is referred to in the West as the 'agricultural and consumer-goods lobby'. In such conditions specialists may then, as previously, be called upon to execute policies laid down by top Party leaders successful in domestic political struggle but possibly inexperienced in international affairs. Indeed, it would not be the first time that well-informed and well-meaning experts *nolens volens* are put in the service of expansionist, imperialist or missionary policies with whose main content and direction they may disagree.[58] (In this connection one may wonder about Anatoly Gromyko's true role in shaping Soviet policy in Africa. Given the character of this policy as a mixture of global power policy and world-revolutionary aspirations it is difficult to decide whether his expert advice merely serves to make this policy more effective and successful, or whether his advice is contrary to current Soviet policy and hence falls on deaf ears.)

Another factor worthy of consideration when thinking about the likely direction of future foreign policy making in the Soviet Union is the current upgrading of the role of the security apparatus and the increase in its power, profile and representation. This is manifest not only in the representation of the KGB in the Politburo (since 1973) but also in the increased number of candidate members of the CC (since 1976) and the promotion of former KGB or internal security chiefs to leading posts in the Union republics, including the post of First Secretary (Aliyev in Azerbaidzhan and Shevardnadze in Georgia). It shows up on official occasions (e.g. the number of representatives of the KGB and the Ministry for Internal Affairs present at the airport honouring Brezhnev's departure or return from abroad)[59] and it is indicated by the fact that a considerable number of KGB officials occupy leading positions in the Foreign and Foreign Trade Ministries (a proportion estimated as being six to four!)[60]

Similarly, it is useful to temper views of the ascendancy of academic specialists in policy making by the observation that their role is likely to be limited when it comes to questions connected with the military dimension of foreign policy. Until recently, there did not even exist a group of civilian scholars comparable to the large community of strategic analysts in the USA. Although this has changed to a certain extent it is still sobering to contemplate the state of affairs as it existed during the SALT I negotiations. The Ministry of Foreign Affairs provided the chairman of the Soviet SALT delegation, and could draw on expertise from sections on disarmament in the Division of International Organisations, the American desk and the Policy Planning Staff, but its role was largely confined to the political aspects of the problem. On the military aspects it had to rely on what it could derive from Western sources.[61] Similar constraints on Foreign Ministry negotiators made themselves felt in the talks in Vienna on mutual force reductions in Central Europe.[62] From all this it is fair to conclude that the Ministry of Defence, primarily through its General Staff, in conjunction with the Party leadership was playing a dominant role in both instances in defining the content of the Soviet position.

This also goes to show that the Party chooses its specialists carefully and, when it does so, has no intention of abandoning its 'leading role'. It is appropriate, therefore, to give due weight to Brezhnev's disclosure in an interview with US journalists in 1973 that when he is away either Suslov or Kirilenko usually presided in Politburo meetings. As Suslov is effectively the Second Secretary of the Central Committee of the CPSU, and Kirilenko *de facto* the Third Secretary, it gives the Party much greater control over decision making than if (as had been assumed) Kosygin in his capacity as head of the state apparatus, or Podgorny in his then capacity as nominal head of state, had fulfilled that function. It is also worth mentioning in this context that leading officials of the domestic Party administrative hierarchy are typically chosen to fill important posts, including those at ambassadorial level, in the 'fraternal countries' of the Warsaw Pact and Comecon, and in other countries where Marxist-Leninist parties are in power.

The reluctance of the Party to entrust too much responsibility to professionals was epitomised at the end of 1977 by the appointment of a 'duumvirate' of First Deputy Foreign Ministers after a vacancy had been created by the promotion of V.V. Kuznetsov to the Presidium of the Supreme Soviet.[63] Of the two appointees, Georgii M. Kornienko and Viktor F. Mal'tsev, the former has undoubtedly a better claim to succeed Gromyko in the post of foreign minister (and in the Politburo?). Kornienko, now 53 years old, joined the Foreign Ministry in 1949, served in various posts at the Soviet embassy in Washington, became head of the USA Department in the USSR Foreign Ministry in 1966 and a Deputy Foreign Minister in October 1975, and has attended all the important bilateral negotiations with the United States in recent years. In contrast, Mal'tsev — who is 61 years old and a full member of the CPSU Central Committee — graduted from the Novosibirsk Institute of Railway Engineers in 1941, held various posts on the Krasnoyarsk, Far Eastern, and East Siberian railroads and was then assigned to Party work as a secretary in the Irkutsk Party Committee (1961-63 and 1965). His experience in foreign policy is quite limited and confined mainly to various ambassadorial posts since the late 1960s.[64] But pointedly, comparison of the respective careers shows that whereas Kornienko has the better professional qualifications, Mal'tsev has the better Party credentials. Time will tell whose career was ultimately more successful. For the time being it is interesting to note that expertise by itself does not constitute the sole criterion of advancement.

In the final analysis, future foreign policy making is likely to be determined by the role of the Party in Soviet society and politics. The Party has proven remarkably resilient and adaptable in the past sixty years of its rule and for all its current emphasis on the 'scientific-technological revolution' and 'scientific' decision making is unlikely to step aside now and voluntarily accept a lesser role. Trends of professionalisation and specialisation in foreign policy making have often been considered as conforming to the (above-mentioned) general diagnosis that the Soviet body politic is being attacked by the virus of de-ideologisation, leading to a sapping of the strength of Marxism-Leninism and a reduction in the leading role of the Party, and ending in some form of pluralism and autonomy for various social and political groups. It is doubtful whether this will happen, or happen soon.

Notes

[1] The concern of the Soviet leadership with the lack of progress in the economic sphere, and in productivity in particular, was reflected in an unprecedented (in the view of this writer) letter issued jointly by the Central Committee of the CPSU, the USSR Council of Ministers, the Trade Unions and the KOMSOMOL and addressed to all the workers and organisations engaged in production, exhorting them to make greater efforts to fulfil and overfulfil production targets. The letter was published prominently in the Soviet newspapers, e.g. *Pravda*, 14 January 1978. In the words of *The Economist* of 4 February 1978 it was almost as if the Queen, the Archbishop of Canterbury, the Labour prime minister, the general secretary of the Trades Union Congress and the Boy Scouts had addressed a joint letter to the working people of Britain urging everybody 'to sin less, pray more and work harder'. Concerning the decline in productivity, the CIA has estimated that the decline amounted to 0.2 per cent annually over the five years from 1971-75: Edgar Ulsamer, 'CIA's Soviet Market Forecast: Mixed', *Air Force Magazine* (November 1976), p. 65.

[2] V.I. Lenin, *Sochineniya* (4th, Russian ed.), XV, p. 67.

[3] The concept of 'congruence' is Alexander Dallin's and its relevance will be considered below, pp. 34-7.

[4] The best examples of such discussion were in the 1950s and 1960s, in particular Chapter 17, 'The Relations of Ideology and Foreign Policy', of Barrington Moore's *Soviet Politics: The Dilemma of Power* (Boston; Mass.: Harvard University Press, 1950); the debate between Richard Lowenthal, Samuel Sharp and R.N. Carew Hunt in *Problems of Communism*, VII, 2 (March-April 1958), pp. 10-30, and ibid., VII, 3 (May-June 1958) pp. 50-52; Zbigniew Brzezinski, *Ideology and Power in Soviet Politics* (New York: Praeger, 1962); and Alfred G. Meyer, 'The Functions of Ideology in the Soviet Political System', *Soviet Studies*, SVII, 3 (January 1966), pp. 273-85.

[5] As part of this thesis of the 'erosion of ideology', William Zimmerman has advocated the view that Soviet and Western perspectives on the international system are essentially similar, see his *Soviet Perspectives on International Relations, 1956-1967* (Princeton, N.J.: Princeton University Press, 1969); 'Soviet Policy in the 1970's', *Survey*, XIX, 2 (Spring 1973), esp. pp. 193-94; and 'Elite Perspectives and the Explanation of Soviet Foreign Policy', *Journal of International Affairs*, XV, 1 (1970), pp. 84-98.

[6] This is a point made by Alexander Yanov, *Detente after Brezhnev: The Domestic Roots of Soviet Foreign Policy*, Policy Papers in International Affairs (Berkeley, Calif.: Institute of International Studies, 1977).

[7] Stalin, *Sochineniya*, X, p. 45.

[8] Steklov in *Izvestiya*, 15 March 1918, as quoted by E.H. Carr, *The Bolshevik Revolution*, III, Pt. 5 (Harmondsworth: Penguin Books, 1971), p. 79.

[9] Vernon Aspaturian has expressed this as follows: 'Soviet ideology itself

defines 'national interest', 'power', and 'world revolution' in such a way as to make them virtually as indistinguishable and inseparable as the three sides of an equlateral triangle'; see his 'Ideology and National Interest in Soviet Foreign Policy', in id., *Process and Power in Soviet Foreign Policy* (Boston: Little, Brown and Company, 1971), p. 331.

[10] Alfred G. Meyer, 'USSR Incorporated', *Slavic Review*, XX (October 1961) pp. 369-76, *vide*, p. 370; similar views are expressed in his *The Soviet Political System* (New York: Random House, 1965). This reference as quoted by Jerry W.F. Hough, 'The Bureaucratic Model and the Nature of the Soviet System', *Journal of Comparative Administration* V, 2 (August 1973), pp. 13-67, *vide* p. 135. An analysis of Western views on Soviet bureaucracy can be found in Hough's article.

[11] T.H. Rigby, 'Hough on Political Participation in the Soviet Union', *Soviet Studies*, XXVIII, 2 (April 1976), pp. 257-61, *vide* p. 258.

[12] Ibid.

[13] Alex Nove, 'History, Hierarchy and Nationalities: Some Observations on the Soviet Social Structure', *Soviet Studies*, XXI, 1 (July 1969), pp. 71-92, *vide* p. 76.

[14] In her contribution to *Sowjetunion 1976-77: Analyse und Bilanz*, the Yearbook on Soviet affairs edited under the auspices of the Bundesinstitut für ostwissenschaftliche und internationale Studien, Cologne. The following summary is essentially a condensed version of A. von Borcke's article.

[15] Brezhnev in *Voprosy istorii KPSS*, No. 12 (1976), p. 107, as quoted in ibid.

[16] Rigby, 'Hough on Political Participation', p. 258,.

[17] Joel C. Moses, 'Regional Cohorts and Political Mobility in the USSR: The Case of Dnepropetrovsk', *Soviet Union* (Philadelphia), No. 3, Pt. 1 (1976), pp. 63-89, as quoted by von Borcke.

[18] This ends the summary based on Astrid von Borcke's article.

[19] H. Gordon Skilling, 'Interest Groups and Communist Politics: An Introduction', in H. Gordon Skilling and Franklyn Griffiths, *Interest Groups in Soviet Politics* (Princeton, N.J.: Princeton University Press, 1971), p. 13.

[20] Jerry F. Hough, 'The Soviet System: Petrification or Pluralism?', *Problems of Communism*, XXI, 3 (March-April, 1972), pp. 25-45.

[21] Milton C. Lodge, 'Soviet Elite Participatory Attitudes in the Post-Stalin Period', *American Political Science Review*, LXII, 3 (September 1968), pp. 827-39, id., *Soviet Elite Attitudes Since Stalin* (Columbus, Ohio: Bell and Howell, 1969).

[22] This is the aphorism that looms large in Graham T. Allison's bureaucratic politics model, e.g. in his *Essence of Decision: Explaining the Cuban Missile Crisis* (Boston: Little, Brown & Co., 1971), p. 176.

[23] Roman Kolkowicz, *The Soviet Military and the Communist Party* (Princeton, N.J.: Princeton University Press, 1967), p. 21.

[24] *Id.*, 'The Military', in Skilling and Griffiths, eds, *Interest Groups in Soviet Politics*, pp. 135-6.

[25] This writer agrees very much with the line of reasoning adopted by William E. Odom, 'The Party Connection', *Problems of Communism*, XXII, (September-October 1973), pp. 12-26, and by Matthew P. Gallagher and Karl F. Spielmann, Jr, *Soviet Decision-Making for Defense* (New York: Praeger, 1972), pp. 40-3.

[26] This is not to say that the political leadership is prepared to go along with · all of the ambitious and far-reaching plans which Admiral Gorshkov seems to have in mind for the Soviet Navy judging from his article series in *Morskoi sbornik* (1970) and the expanded book version (*Morskaya moshch' qosudarstva*, published in 1976). This is also not to say that the Soviet Navy is now superior to the US Navy in blue-water capabilities. Most of the new Soviet surface vessels are small and capable only of short-range operations. See Michael MccGwire, 'Soviet Naval Programmes', *Survival*, No. 5 (1973), pp. 218-27; id., 'Western and Soviet Naval Building Programmes, 1965-1976', in ibid., No. 5 (1976), pp. 204-9; and id., (ed.), *Soviet Naval Influence* (New York: Praeger, 1977), esp. pp. 612-52. See also Geoffrey Jukes, 'Das Problem der Uberalterung der Schiffe in der sowjetischen Marine', *Marine-Rundschau*, No. 1 (1977), pp. 4-9.

[27] Prior to Ustinov's appointment there were only two exceptions to the general practice of appointing military officers to the post of Defence Minister, Trotsky and Bulganin.

[28] This problem is explored further in Hannes Adomeit and Mikhail Agursky, *The Soviet Military-Industrial Complex and Its Internal Mechanism*, Research Paper published in the National Security Series, Centre for International Relations, Queen's University, Kingston, Ontario, No. 1/1978. See also Karl F. Spielmann, 'Defense Industrialists in the USSR', *Problems of Communism*, XXV, 5 (September-October 1976), pp. 52-69.

[29] Zhukov was said to have: (1) plotted the overthrow of the regime; (2) disagreed on policy matters with civilian leaders; (3) sponsored a 'cult of his own personality'; (4) administered the military establishment in an 'incorrect and non-Party manner'; and (5) attacked the military Party organs; see Timothy J. Coulton, 'The Zhukov Affair Reconsidered', *Soviet Studies*, XXIX, 2 (April 1977), pp. 158-213, *vide* p. 190.

[30] Ibid., pp. 212-13.

[31] Ibid., p. 212.

[32] Kolkowicz, 'The Military', in Skilling and Griffiths (eds), *Interest Groups in Soviet Politics*, p. 141.

[33] Ilana Dimant-Kass, 'The Soviet Military and Soviet Policy in the Middle East 1970-73', *Soviet Studies*, XXVI, 4 (October 1974), pp. 502-21, *vide* pp. 520-1.

[34] Ibid., p. 512. In the quest to establish the strong role of the military in foreign policy making one analyst goes even as far as venturing the thesis that the

military has been able to turn international crises off and on so as to check trends for a reduction in defence spending: Raymond Hutchings, 'Soviet Defence Spending and Soviet External Relations', *International Affairs* (London), ILVII (1971), pp. 5181-31.

[35] Malcolm Mackintosh, 'The Soviet Military: Influence on Foreign Policy' *Problems of Communism*, XXII, 5 (September-October 1973), pp. 10-11.

[36] To take but one example of a contrary line of argument. One author writes that 'during the 1957 Syrian crisis, when Baghdad Pact forces threatened to invade Syria to prevent an alleged takeover by the Communist Party there, Zhukov, in an unauthorised statement over Albanian radio, declared the Soviet military's readiness "to strike at any military adventure organised by the United States near our southern borders". Almost immediately after, Khrushchev appeared unexpectedly at a Soviet-Turkish reception, announcing that the Syrian conflict should be resolved peacefully and that Marshal Zhukov had been relieved of all his posts.' Karen Dawisha, 'The Limits of the Bureaucratic Politics Model: Observations on the Soviet Case', Paper delivered to the Annual Conference of BNASEES, Cambridge, 26-28 March 1977, p. 4. Whether or not Zhukov's statement was unauthorised is a mere conjecture. On the other hand a statement like the one quoted from Zhukov's speech is not at all unusual but typical of the kind of statement that characterised the Khrushchev eta. Certainly, it would be erroneous to characterise Zhukov as an adventurist in foreign policy.

[37] Such a line of reasoning is attributed to the Soviet military by William E. Odom in 'The Soviet Military and Foreign Policy', *Survival*, XVII, 6 (November/December 1975), pp. 276-81.

[38] The power and role of the first *obkom* secretaries has been compared to that of the French prefects by Jerry Hough, *The Soviet Prefects* (Cambridge, Mass.: Harvard University Press, 1969). It is necessary to clarify, however, that Hough (who kindly commented on the draft of this contribution) is not to be counted among those who share the 'broad agreement' concerning the role of the *obkom* Secretaries. In his view, the Secretaries are advocates of economic reform because such reform would bring more money into the *oblast*', and they would be in a position to influence its allocation.

[39] See, for instance, William J. Conyngham, *Industrial Management in the Soviet Union: The Role of the CPSU in Industrial Decision-making, 1917-1970* (Stanford, Calif.: Hoover Institution Press,1973), p. 285.

[49] Yanov, *Detente after Brezhnev*, op. cit. (see fn. 6 above), pp. 29-30.

[41] Ibid., p.30.

[42] *Sowjetunion 1976-77*, op. cit. (see fn. 14 above).

[43] See the table compiled by Dawisha, 'The Limits of the Bureaucratic Politics Model', op. cit. (see fn. 36 above), p. 10.

[44] Stephen L. White, 'Contradiction and Change in State Socialism', *Soviet Studies*, XXVI, 1 (January 1974), p. 42.

[45] That there *can* be a positive correlation between reformism and interna-

46

tional economic interdependence in communist countries was demonstrated in Czechoslovakia during the Dubcek era.

[46] Alexander Dallin, 'Domestic Factors Influencing Soviet Foreign Policy', in Michael Confino and Shimon Shamir, *The USSR and the Middle East* (Jerusalem: Israel University Press, 1973), pp. 5-30, *vide* p. 32.

[47] This is expressed in the article as quoted in the previous reference and, more systematically, in his earlier article, 'Soviet Foreign Policy and Domestic Politics: A Framework for Analysis', *Journal of International Affairs*, XXIII, 2 (1969), pp. 250-65.

[48] Vernon Aspaturian, 'Moscow's Options in a Changing World', *Problems of Communism*, XXI, 4 (July-August 1962), pp. 1-20, *vide* p. 6.

[49] Dallin, 'Domestic Factors Influencing Soviet Foreign Policy', p. 47.

[50] Victor Zorza, writing about the Politburo's problem in dealing with Sakharov. The full citation reads: 'As on every other major issue, there are differences in the Kremlin itself between hardliners and moderates on how to deal with this matter'. *International Herald Tribune*, 14 October 1975.

[51] Convincing evidence to this effect is given by Uri Ra'anan, *The USSR Arms the Third World: Case Studies in Soviet Foreign Policy* (Cambridge, Mass.: The MIT Press, 1969).

[52] For example, by Terry McNeill in Radio Liberty Research, RL299/74, 20 September 1974.

[53] See, for instance, Boris Rabbot, 'A Letter to Brezhnev', in *The New York Times Magazine*, 6 November 1977, p. 55. Rabbot was a Secretary of the of the Social Science Section of the Presidium of the Academy of Sciences of the USSR and adviser to the CC.

[54] This listing is based on Jerry F. Hough, 'The Coming Generational Change in the Soviet Foreign Policy-Making Elite', Paper Presented to the National Convention of AAASS, 14 October 1977, pp. 1-3.

[55] Ibid., pp. 6-7.

[56] *Pravda*, 15 October 1976.

[57] For more detail concerning the issue of professionalisation and specialisation, and its potential significance for future foreign policy making, see ibid., pp. 9-32.

[58] Without wanting to commit the error of equalising Soviet and Nazi foreign policy, it is useful to remember that the major portion of the German Foreign Ministry under Hitler was opposed to the NSDAP's disastrous policies in international affairs. However, its power was insufficient to affect a change of course.

[59] For instance, five KGB and MVD (Ministry for Internal Affairs) representatives appeared at Vnukovo airport to see Brezhnev off: Andropov (Chairman of the KGB), S.K. Tsvigun (First Deputy Chairman of the KGB), G.K. Tsinev (Deputy Chairman of the KGB), N.A. Shchelokov (head of MVD) and Yu.M. Churbanov (Chief of the Political Administration of the MVD Internal

Forces); *Pravda*, 21 June 1977.

[60] Estimates of the Rockefeller Commission; see also *International Herald Tribune*, 24 December 1975.

[61] See Marshall D. Shulman's discussion in *Survey*, XIX, 2 (Spring 1973), pp. 177-8 and the article by Raymond Garthoff, 'SALT and the Soviet Military', *Problems of Communism*, (January-February 1975).

[62] According to information obtained through a member of the British delegation in Vienna. However, much of this may be a thing of the past. More recent (confidental) information indicates that Soviet civilian negotiators at such high-level talks as SALT II, and presumably also the later stages of M(B)FR, now know about 90 per cent of what the military knows.

[63] For the announcement see *Pravda*, 24 December 1977. Kuznetsov had been promoted to First Deputy Chairman of the Supreme Soviet in October 1977.

[64] See Radio Liberty Research (Bulletin), RL 1/78, 1 January 1978, esp. the Appendix. To point out the complexities of the problem, Hough argues (in a review of the draft of this contribution) that the appointment of two or more first deputy ministers is not unusual where the number of deputy ministers increases in a ministry, say, where it reaches the level of about seven to eight. (At the latest count there were nine deputy ministers in the Soviet foreign ministry. In the ministry of defence, where there are 12-13 deputy ministers, three are listed as first.) As to the appointment of Mal'tsev and Kornienko, his argument continues, it is quite possible that it was at least in part determined by considerations of specialisation, Mal'tsev to deal with problems of the Third World, Kornienko with those of the capitalist countries, and that, although the former has the better formal Party credentials, Kornienko has the better (informal) access to leading members of the Central Committee apparatus and the Politburo. The difficulties of interpretation remain.

3 Socialism, nationalism and underdevelopment: research on Romanian foreign policy making

JEANNE KIRK LAUX

Introduction

The most striking feature of Romania's foreign policy making is its apparent independence. If Romania has captured an inordinate amount of Western press attention since 1964, it is not because a great many people are fascinated by the innate historical processes of Romanian development, but because they look at Romania as belonging to a special class of states — socialist states ruled by Marxist-Leninist parties — and as a particular sub-type of socialist state — small and relatively less developed.[1] The Romanian leadership was the first to demonstrate clearly that the foreign policy conduct of a small socialist state was not exclusively a function of Soviet prescriptions, despite formal alignment with the Soviet Union, and that its definition of the international situation was not imitatively deduced from Marxism-Leninism but rather modified according to national realities. Other Marxist-Leninist ruling parties, it is true, had already redefined ideology in order to differentiate their national experiences from the Soviet model and had also extended these differences to the realm of interstate relations. But unlike the Romanian party, the Yugoslav, Chinese and Albanian parties came to power without heavy reliance on the Soviet Union and are not today full members of either the Soviet sponsored economic (Comecon) or military (Warsaw Treaty Organisation) alliances.

Romania first made international headlines by refusing to conform to Soviet preferences for regional economic integration within Comecon and then moved into the diplomatic limelight by casting its vote differently from its allies on arms control issues in the United Nations (1965). Dramatic breaks from established Warsaw Pact policy in 1967-68 — recognition of West Germany, refusal to condemn Israeli 'aggression' and denunciation of its allies' military intervention in Czechoslovakia — reinforced Romania's maverick image. Romanian initiatives in international economic policy continue to distinguish the country from other European Comecon member states in the 1970s; in return, Romania gained special preferences from the European Common Market based on its self-declared status as a less developed country and reconfirmed

49

the identity when it joined UNCTAD 77, the caucus group of developing countries.

Romania's international behaviour is still closely watched today — seen by some as an indicator of the extent of ideological differentiation among socialist states and by others as a test of the autonomy permissible for small states in hierarchical alliance systems. The study of Romanian foreign policy making thus requires a comparative framework of analysis wherein we can situate the similarities and differences between Romania and other ruling Marxist-Leninist parties; other small states in alliance; or other rapidly industrialising peasant societies. In order, for example, to understand why Romania moved from apparent conformity to initiate an independent foreign policy in the early 1960s, we need to move beyond descriptive case studies and to ask the kind of exciting analytical questions that can only be answered by comparative study. Three main questions will be used to guide the rest of this study: What are the conditions which account for (1) variation across states of the same class and (2) variation across time for the same state and (3) What, empirically, is the degree of deviation by *one* state from the collective pattern of foreign policy behaviour of *all* socialist states?

In this contribution to the anthology, questions of methodology will be discussed as they emerge from a concrete analysis of Romanian foreign policy in two important issue-areas: economic cooperation and military security. Limiting attention to contemporary (post-1960) Romania and to comparison with the most similar states belonging to the Warsaw Pact, I will draw on the work of Western specialists on Romania in order to distill the principal factors which may account for Romania's divergent foreign policy.[2] Using the three broad comparative questions posed above, we want to know more specifically why Romania alone challenged Soviet preferences for the reorganisation of Comecon, moving instead to initiate an independent interpretation of socialist foreign policy, and why Romania's foreign policy orientation then shifted from militant nationalism, especially on military security questions, to a more adaptive strategy of selective cooperation. Finally, we want to specify just how different is Romania's external behaviour in the 1970s when compared to that of other small communist countries. The answers to these questions will bring out those similarities and differences between Romania and other communist states as regards historical setting, the role of the Party and the role of ideology in foreign policy making.

The policy makers in the six allied socialist states share a common reality, as Barry Farrell has emphasised. They are leaders of small states in a region dominated by a superpower, the Soviet Union. As a consequence, all have had to deal with the problem of somehow defining the boundaries of their own authority in policy making as distinct from the Soviet Union's perceived area of interest.[3] Exactly how they have done so has varied across states and across time, but all must recognise that the consequences of misinterpreting this boundary can be disastrous — as the intervention in Czechoslovakia once again demonstrated. The Soviet Union cannot be regarded as simply another, rather large external actor in the neighbourhood. As Party state leaders, formally sharing the Marxist-Leninist premise of proletarian internationalism, all East European policy makers also must operate within an institutionalised network of inter-party relations more hierarchical than egalitarian. Given disparities in economic and military size, and the Soviet leadership's expectation that pre-war deference to the first ruling Party should continue, both inter-state and inter-Party relations remain unequal. Until at least 1960 all socialist policies in Eastern Europe qualified as 'penetrated systems' — here I refer to James Rosenau's concept. In his view,

> A penetrated political system is one in which non-members of a national society participate directly and authoritatively through actions taken jointly with the society's members, in either the allocation of its values or the mobilization of support on behalf of its goals.[4]

The geopolitical and institutional setting in Eastern Europe results in a symbiotic relationship between domestic politics and foreign policy which should become clear during our discussion of Romanian foreign policy making. The Romanian political élite's effort to define its own area of authority differs from that of other small socialist states in being both more articulate and more successful.

The basic objective of Romanian foreign policy since at least 1962 can be succinctly summarised under the heading of 'national autonomy'. By national autonomy I mean, following Richard Cooper, 'the ability to frame and carry out objectives . . . which may diverge widely from those of other countries'.[5] The pursuit of national autonomy as practised by Romanian foreign policy makers calls for two complementary strategies. Firstly, Romania seeks to minimise those forms of collaboration within Soviet-sponsored institutions which would diminish sovereignty — by which I mean, again following Cooper, 'the formal ability of countries to make their own decisions and to renounce previously made decisions'.[6] Initially, this strategy took militant form with flamboyant unilateral postures designed to emphasise national priorities, whereas since 1970-71 a more tempered approach to relations with socialist partners underlies the practice of selective cooperation. Secondly, Romania seeks to diversify external ties with both socialist states (outside the Warsaw Pact) and non-socialist states. Diversification serves at once a protective and a promotive purpose — avoiding isolation, and thus inhibiting Soviet sanctions, while augmenting national economic capabilities and thereby reducing the extent of necessary reliance on regional partners. Romania's revision of Marxist-Leninist ideology legitimised diversification and justifies national autonomy. Since 1964 the new credo centralises the role of the state and elevates the authority of national parties while it emphasises those state attributes (such as small size) which transect socio-economic systems.

Why different?

Romania's independent foreign policy began with a confrontation over economic cooperation. The Romanian party leadership refused to accept Khrushchev's 1962 prescriptions for the reorganisation of Comecon along lines of supranationality to achieve integration through specialisation of industries across member countries.[7] This mode of industrial specialisation represented a shift in regional development strategy away from the classic Leninist-Stalinist model — favouring rapid accumulation and reinvestment in the leading sectors of heavy industry to promote 'socialism in one country' — toward regionally coordinated planning to rationalise existing industries, a strategy preferred by the more industrialised states, especially Czechoslovakia and the GDR.[8] Romania objected both to the content of the proposals on economic integration, which would have entailed abandoning plans for industrial development already under-way, and to the political form of cooperation, which would have imposed majority solutions on the minority. Unable to convince its partners during multinational bargaining in Comecon to retain Stalinist development priorities and then unable to persuade the Soviet Union (1962-1964) to subsidise Romania's steel industry despite new Comecon priorities, the Romania's steel industry despite new Comecon priorities, the Romanian leadership chose nonetheless to pursue its preordained rapid industrialisation programme.

In the first instance, then, Romania did not initiate an independent foreign policy but sought to preserve a favourable international situation in reaction to policy initiatives taken by other party states. Determined to carry out goals of national development, which now diverged from the objectives of others, the Romanian leadership legitimised this choice by deriving an appropriate set of ideological principles — the April 1964 'Declaration of Independence' — to guide future relations with the socialist party states. In order therefore to answer our first question (why did Romania evolve an independent foreign policy orientation?) we actually need to answer three subsidiary questions: Why did Romania's development priorities differ from those of other small socialist partners? Why did the Romanian political élite choose to pursue a divergent strategy rather than defer to its allies' preferences? And finally, why should a narrow confrontation over industrialisation have been extrapolated into a general foreign policy orientation?

David Lane reminds us 'that Marxist-Leninist parties, which all share more or less similar values, come to power in societies which already have their own cultural values and are at differing levels of economic development'. Comparative research should be able to 'bring out their varying cultural character or historical experience and its impact on the socio-political system copied from or imposed by the Soviet Union'.[9] Level of economic development appears to be the determining factor accounting for different development priorities among Comecon member states in the 1960s.[10] The Romanian Communist Party took power in a society which ranked among the least developed in Europe, according to economic indicators (e.g. share of industry in national income, proportion of population actively employed in agriculture, agricultural productivity, and share of manufactures in exports) as well as social indicators (e.g. literacy, infant mortality, life expectancy, and caloric consumption).[11] Official Comecon development priorities in the 1950s, based on the Soviet model, had suited Romanian socio-economic conditions. When the Romanian political élites decided at the Party Congress in 1960 to mobilise resources for completing the development of major industrial sectors and the collectivisation of agriculture they merely sought to reiterate the Soviet experience after 1928.

Awareness of Romania's low level of economic development permits us to understand the élite's preference for retaining the Leninist-Stalinist model of development when faced with new proposals for regional integration better suited to the needs of specialisation in the advanced industrial states in Comecon. But although Bulgaria shared with Romania a similar legacy of industrial underdevelopment, the Bulgarian élite opted for compliance to new Comecon norms thereby accepting a future in which agriculture would play a major role in economic growth.[12] Clearly other factors must be considered if we want to account for the Romanian political élite's tenacity. When we compare Romania to Bulgaria in an effort to explain the respective motivations of political élites in the area of economic development policy, two contrasting historical experiences emerge. Different patterns of rural development created different class structures, engendering an antipathy to the peasantry in Romanian élite culture which has carried over to the communist élite. Differences in direct experience with the USSR during wartime reconstruction undermined the Romanian Communist Party's trust in Soviet solidarity.

The pattern of Turkish colonialism and the corresponding structure of land ownership at the time of independence in Romania contrast sharply with the Bulgarian experience. In Romania, indirect Turkish rule permitted consolidation of enormous estates and 'thus the development of capitalist agriculture which took place in Romania chiefly under the leadership of the commodity-producing large estates followed the pattern in the countries east of the Elbe instead of displaying any similarity to that in the Balkan countries'.[13] In Bulgaria, direct rule retained the established small-holder land ownership pattern and at independence, just as throughout the interwar period, Bulgaria had the most egalitarian distribution of land of any of the future Comecon member states. Its peasant farming system has been seen as a 'perfect counterpart of the development which took place in Great Britain'.[14] (In both states during the interwar period, it is true, a commercial bourgeoisie, or its military agents, held state power and acted as a clientele class in collaboration with international capital. Investment patterns thus favoured export-oriented industry to the neglect of agriculture). The traditional upper and middle class attitudes of contempt for the squalid peasant life persisted in socialist Romania in the form of a total rejection of reliance on agriculture. Cultural legacy combined with Soviet norms to convince the RCP élite that rapid industrialisation was the only acceptable mode of development.[15]

Direct experience with the Soviet Party *apparatchiki* in the immediate postwar period is the second historical factor presumed to have influenced the Romanian party élite's tenacity in pursuing a semi-autarkic economic development model. The Soviet Union regarded both Romania and Bulgaria (and Hungary) as enemy belligerents. Even after the dissolution of coalition government and nationalisation compaigns had brought these states into the circle of Socialist allies, the Soviets continued to extract heavy war reparations. The relative severity of Soviet extractive economic policy in the Balkans is seen by some authors to have affected the relative pro- or anti-Russian attitudes, with Bulgaria perceived to be a friendly Slavic nation and Romania a traditional antagonist. However, the economic costs of Soviet reparations were perhaps less significant than the psychological-political impact of Soviet policy in generating a latent mistrust of Soviet intentions on the part of the Romanian communist leadership. J.M. Montias, a leading western economist studying Romanian development, concluded:

> 'I am well aware that political issues probably strained Romania's relations with the Soviet Union more seriously than did any economic factors. ... These political issues include the annexation of Bessarabia in 1940, the imposition of a heavy reparation burden on a country that considered herself an ally of the Soviet Union in the last nine months of World War II, the exploitation of Romania resources by the mixed companies, the stinting aid given to Romania for her industrialization, and the humiliating political subservience imposed by their Soviet mentors . . .'[17]

Pursuit of a semi-autarkic policy to achieve rapid industralisation had originally been sanctioned by official Soviet Marxism, but the Romanian élite's motivation to retain this policy gained strong reinforcement both from traditional cultural biases and direct experience with Soviet officials. The capacity of the Romanian political élite to carry out its preferred development strategy despite Soviet opposition can be seen as a function of two types of factors. The principal internal factor singled out by Western specialists on Romania is Party institutionalisation (itself explained by reference to inherited political culture and to leadership). The principal external variable is the international balance of forces, especially relations of conflict or collaboration between the major powers which posed constraints or offered opportunities for policy initiation.

Kenneth Jowitt contends that faced with the necessity for choice in 1962 (and in contrast to Bulgaria), 'the Romanian regime possessed a relatively united élite, a coherent organisation . . . Possessing a political character of this order, it accepted the conflict over industrialisation as an opportunity, with the result that the Romanian party was strengthened in its capacity to exercise political ideological initiative'.[18] Credit for Party institutionalisation in Romania goes to the First Party Secretary, Gheorghiu-Dej, but Dej's success is explained by reference to both regime and mass political culture. The Romanian party élite drew its 'operational code' from Russian Marxism rather than German social-democratic traditions in the nineteenth century, and exclusive association with the Russian Party later reinforced a dirigiste version of socialism according to Jacques Levesque's interpretation.[19] Jowitt demonstates how Dej exploited the congruity between traditional peasant values and Stalinist bureaucratic norms to build up a patrimonial party by massive recruitment (over 800,000 members in 1960) with cadres personally dependent on Dej's patronage.[20]

'One might hypothesize', Jowitt then argues, 'that the stability of Dej's regime was partially due to the congruence between the structure and ethos of his rule and the historical experience, social composition and notion of authority held by large sectors of Romanian society'.[21] The tiny middle class, the high proportion of illiterate peasant population, the lack of defined organisational forces, like the Catholic Church in Poland, and a traditional political culture emphasising state-society antagonism are all cited as factors permitting the undiluted exercise of Stalinist power to build up the Communist Party's power base.[22] 'The question of legitimacy defined as politically conscious consent was not a major question at all — it presupposes the existence of a participatory constituency and tradition. The situation was quite different in peasant, patriarchal, and authoritarian Romania'.[23]

The Romanian political élite was able to act out its preferred development strategy (as reflected in the decision taken at the plenum of the Executive Committee in December 1963) to pursue rapid industrialisation, thanks not only to internal cohesion but also to favourable external conditions created by the tensions between the Soviet Union and China. China's challenge to Soviet ideological domination presented an opportunity to enhance national autonomy while obviating Soviet reprisals. Levesque has skilfully chronicled Soviet-Romanian-Chinese relations, showing how Romania consistently supported the USSR in polemics with the Chinese Party until mid-1962 when Khrushchev announced his plans for Comecon integration.[24] Faced with the loss of Soviet support, the Romanians first dropped direct references to China (or Albania), then began to decry all condemnations of any fraternal party, offering to play a mediating role between Moscow and Peking. The Romanian ploy was initially successful. In June 1963, when China presented a 25 point list of conditions for reconciliation to the Central Committee of the CPSU, it included as point 21 a denunciation of Comecon integration plans. Comecon supranationality was not only attacked as being an imitation of capitalism (the EEC) but also as an intolerable abuse of the socialist state which wished to pursue self-reliant development.[25] The following month, at the meeting of party leaders from Comecon member countries, Khrushchev decided to postpone the reorganisation of Comecon.

Very rapidly, however, a sharp deterioration in Sino-Soviet relations induced the Romanian leadership to extend its apparent victory on the issue of economic integration into a protective nationalist revision of Marxism-Leninism to guide foreign policy in the future. When the Romanian attempt to reconcile the Soviet and Chinese parties during the summer of 1963 failed, the Soviet leadership sought to mobilise support to excommunicate China from the international communist movement and to reconsolidate Soviet power within Europe.[26] The consequent loss of opportunities for manoeuvre provoked Romania's 'Declaration of Independence', which Levesque sees as 'an effort at clarification, justification, and systematization of Romanian foreign policy. . . . since 1962'.[27]

Ideology plays a vital role in Romanian foreign policy making. It is often said that the function of official ideology in domestic politics is to mask social contradictions in order to generalise the particular interests of the dominant social group. Similarly, the Romanian political elite drew upon Leninism as a source for operational principles in international politics in order to mask contradictions by emphasising the broad community of fourteen socialist states (all paths to communism adopted by them being legitimate) and to generalise national interests by presenting socialist patriotism as synonymous with proletarian internationalism. The basic principles set out in the Declaration remain the basis for Romanian foreign policy making today, despite change in the top leadership and despite changes in the international setting which have engendered modifications and extrapolations from the original text.

In its Declaration the RCP justified its refusal to accept the reorganisation of Comecon. 'The idea of a single planning body for all CMEA countries has the most serious economic and political implications. The planned management of the national economy is one of the fundamental, essential, and inalienable attributes of the sovereignty of the socialist state — the state plan being the chief means through which the socialist state achieves political and socio-economic objectives. . . . Transmitting such levers to the competence of superstate or extrastate bodies would turn sovereignty into a meaningless notion'. Recalling that other parties had rationalised Comecon supranationality by reference to Lenin's dictum that there would ultimately be a world-wide socialist economy, the RCP countered with citations from Lenin 'according to which the states and the national distinctions will be maintained until the world-wide victory of socialism and even a long time after it'.

The conclusion was clear: 'Bearing in mind the diversity of the conditions of socialist construction, there are not nor can there be any unique pattern and recipes. . . . It is up to every Marxist-Leninist party, it is a sovereign right of each socialist state, to elaborate, choose, or change the forms and methods of socialist construction'. In any case, since 'there are 14 socialist countries in the world and only some of them are CMEA members', inclusive rather than exclusive forms of cooperation were called for. The autonomy of each party, according to the Romanian élite, could serve the solidarity of all in the 'historical competition between capitalism and socialism' since 'in the nature of the socialist system there are no objective causes for contradictions between the national and international tasks of the socialist countries, between the interests of each country and the interests of the socialist community as a whole'.[28]

Conflict over industrial development was thus extended to create a new ideology of international relations among socialist states. The operative principles invoked in the Romanian statement, and reiterated in virtually all official statements thereafter — state sovereignty, territorial integrity, equal rights, noninterference in internal affairs — do not represent doctrinal innovation (having been set out by Khrushchev in his attempted reconciliation with Tito, used by Mao and enshrined in the Warsaw Pact treaty), but rather a political challenge coming from a small and previously subordinate party state within the alliance.[29]

Variation over time

The pattern of Romanian foreign policy behaviour since the 1964 Declaration has varied over time, and most experts distinguish two principal phases — 'militant nationalism' from 1966-69, and a more quiescent period of 'selective cooperation' after 1970-71. Unfortunately, there has been little systematic effort to monitor Romanian foreign policy outputs; instead, experts rely on interpretation of the exceptional event. Efforts by international relations theorists to create a general empirical typology of foreign policy behaviour are very rudimentary in any case, and typologies of definition 'devised according to the observer's mental model of the distinguishing features of state behaviour' still predominate.[30] Here, too, we must rely on qualitative interpretation to define the two phases and specify the shifting external and domestic conditions which may affect foreign policy making processes and outcomes in Romania. After the hiatus in 1964-65, when the party secretaries changed in both the USSR and Romania, a period of 'militant nationalism' can be identified by reference to flamboyant Romanian decisions in the military security area which diverged from Warsaw Pact collective policy. The four most striking examples are (1) recognition of the German Federal Republic (1967); (2) refusal to condemn Israeli aggression (June 1967); (3) non-ratification of the Nuclear Non-proliferation treaty (1968); and (4) non-participation in and condemnation of the intervention of Czechoslovakia (1968). Militant nationalism took the following forms: unilateralism on international security issues; exposure of attempted Soviet sanctions; diversification of diplomacy outside the bloc; and manipulation of nationalist symbols at home. At the level of ideology, divergence was reflected in emphasis on state sovereignty and combined with a small-state identity to rationalise extra-alliance linkages and deflect Soviet intervention.[31]

In trying to account for Romania's shift from reactive confrontation with the Soviet Union over national development strategy to active provocation over international security policy, we cannot rely on the same factors which helped us to understand why Romania's development priorities differed from those of other small Comecon states. In a short time (and we are talking about the 1960-69 period), factors such as historical experiences or political culture have an invariant impact on policy making.[32] It is useful, therefore, also to turn to more 'conjunctural' factors such as the shifting balance of political forces, both international and domestic. The new Soviet leadership, for example, placed priority on alliance consolidation — first by means of organisational reforms and then by sanctions imposed on Romania for nonconformity — thereby reducing the opportunities for manoeuvre within the regional alliances. Options within the international communist movement were further reduced by China's virtual withdrawal from external relationships during the Cultural Revolution.[33] On the other hand opportunities for extra-bloc relations were enhanced by Soviet-American détente. The shift in superpower relations from confrontation to limited strategic accommodation, usually dated from the Test Ban Treaty in mid-1963, created a permissive environment for the resumption of East-West relations between small European states. The USSR officially endorsed bilateral diplomacy at the Warsaw Pact meeting in Bucharest in July 1966 so as to promote its campaign in favour of a Conference on European Security.[34]

The Romanian leadership interpreted this new international situation differently from the other small socialist states, seeing it through the prism of its revised official ideology which centralised the role of the state and the autonomy of national parties. Soviet intentions (1965-66) of integrating Warsaw Pact forces and coordinating the member states' foreign policies were regarded as unacceptable efforts to subvert state sovereignty.[35] It might be tempting to relate Romania's negative reaction to geopolitical considerations but, of course, Hungary and Bulgaria share a peripheral status with Romania in the military alliance. All three are located in the European southern tier and share the experience of having been allies of the Axis (thus they lack border claims or revanchist fears *vis-à-vis* West Germany). All three have a poor record of Warsaw Pact participation — measured by defence expenditures *per capita* or engagement in joint military manoeuvres — yet only Romania took radical action in response to Soviet proposals.[36]

The new Romanian party secretary, Nicolai Ceausescu, first responded to the Soviet proposals for a reform of the Warsaw Pact with counterproposals, and when these were ignored he lashed out at Moscow in a vehement speech which dates the beginning of the militant nationalist period in Romanian foreign policy (May 1966). Ceausescu degraded the role of the Red Army in Romania's liberation and asserted that 'One of the barriers on the road to cooperation among peoples are the military blocs. . . . (which) represent an anachronism incompatible with the independence and sovereignty of peoples, with normal interstate relations'.[37] Instead he argued that trans-alliance ties between small states and new regional security systems under United Nations auspices offered a better guarantee for peace.[38] This tripartite theme — small-state solidarity, promotion of extra-alliance fora, and vigilance in the face of hegemony (always rationalised by citing the 1964 Declaration) — became a litany in every Romanian foreign policy pronouncement during 1966-69. 'Reality', argued Ceausescu at the ostentatious Grand National Assembly devoted to foreign policy questions, 'shows that solving international divergencies can no longer be decided by the big powers alone. . . . At present an increasing number of small and medium-sized states make their way vigorously and persistently in the arena of world politics and refuse any longer to play the role of pawns in the service of the interests of the big imperialist powers'.[39]

Shifting domestic political forces intervene between international changes and ideological predispositions to explain the degree of militancy in Romania's foreign policy behaviour during 1966-69. The militant nationalist period corresponds to a period of power consolidation by the new leadership. Nicolai Ceausescu used three techniques[40] — personnel manipulation, policy consensus, and populism — each of which was facilitated by publicising external dangers. Exposure of Soviet threats, combined with evocation of national traditions, helped to foster public support for the party and its leader. The regime mobilised historians, poets, and even philologists to proclaim the continuity between the party state and the national past — now as for the past 2,000 years external threats jeopardised the independent development of the Romanian people.[41]

Exposure of Soviet threats also enabled Ceausescu to forge general consensus, eliminate rivals and thus consolidate his personal power within the party apparat. The USSR apparently sought to persuade the new Romanian leadership to return to orthodoxy by imposing several sanctions, including support for a pro-Soviet faction within the party and withholding promised raw materials deliveries in 1967. These efforts were vigorously denounced in public speeches by Ceausescu as he moved to eliminate his major personal rivals from the Dej era and to initiate political reforms to centralise authority.[42] State and party posts were fused in 1967, and Ceausescu took the new position of President himself. By augmenting the Dej Central Committee from 100 to 300 members (including alternates) he built up a cadre structure personally dependent on his patronage. Overall party membership swelled to make the Romanian Communist Party the largest in Eastern Europe as a proportion of population. Ceausescu's accumulation of posts and orchestration of a leadership cult also made the Romanian party the most personalist in Eastern Europe.[43]

The apogee of militant nationalism came in August 1968 when Ceausescu denounced the Pact intervention in Czechoslovakia in a patriotic speech to the people. Having just mobilised the armed forces and created an armed people's militia he now challenged the Soviet Union:

> ... it has been said that in Czechoslovakia a danger of counter-revolution exists; who knows but what tomorrow they will find someone to say that here, too, at this meeting, a counter-revolutionary tendency was revealed? We will answer to all — the entire Romanian people will never allow anyone to invade the territory of our fatherland![44]

And, indeed, although the use of arms was not needed, resistance to Soviet pressures for joint manoeuvres on Romanian soil in spring 1969 required extraordinary diplomatic parrying (including a visit by US President Nixon to Bucharest).[45]

In 1970-71 Romanian foreign policy made a transition from militant nationalism to relative quiescence. Now selective cooperation rather than unilateralism characterised intra-bloc relations; military-security preoccupations receded in favour of economic development issues; and the scope of external relations widened with the promotion of ties to third world nations. Expert definition of this cooperative period relies again on a series of special events — the signature of the Soviet-Romanian friendship treaty; Romania's ratification of the contested nuclear non-proliferation treaty (1970); and its agreement to join the Comecon International Investment Bank despite initial refusal (1971).[46]

A qualitative shift in the conduct of foreign relations suggests that the domestic and external conditions accounting for the prior pattern had changed. James Rosenau writes that in a truly comparative state of mind, 'instead of asking how various things converge to produce a certain set of outcomes in a given society, one asks what are the similarities and differences between this outcome and this process in this situation as against an outcome and a process in another situation'.[47] Looking back to the factors which explained militant nationalism, we find change in two external factors. Opportunities within the international communist movement had expanded with China's return to the international arena in 1970.[48] Opportunities for extra-bloc relations had receded as partial settlement of the outstanding European security issues removed the *raison d'être* for independent East-West diplomacy by a small state.[49] The principal domestic factor cited to explain the degree of militancy was leadership change: nationalism served to consolidate Ceausescu's power position through enhanced party cohesion and popular support. Here we find little change in the 1970s. Although power consolidation was accomplished by the X Party Congress in 1969, experts agree that hierarchical centralisation of institutions and cult of personality have continued apace in the 1970s.[50]

At this point it may be appropriate to interject some observations on conceptual frameworks used to explain the process of foreign policy making and ask whether the high degree of centralism and personalism in Romania implies the absence of conflicting interests in that process. A great deal has already been written on the inadequacies of interest group analysis for the study of politics in communist countries.[51] The interest group tradition stemming from either Bentley or Truman is wedded to conditions found only in pluralist political systems typical of advanced capitalist societies. In state socialist systems, the party's monopoly power and the state's directive role in organising economic and social activity denies independent access to resources needed to articulate interests effectively. (The Romanian Constitution states in Article III that 'the leading force of the whole of society is the Romanian Communist Party' which (Article XXVI) 'directs the activity of the mass and public organisations and of the state bodies'.)

This observation does not deny the existence of fundamental conflicts of interest within state socialist systems. As long as a minority (the party state *apparat*) directs the production process and disposes of surplus value, many theorists feel there is antagonistic conflict of interest between the working class and the *apparat*.[52] Nor does the argument that organised interest groups are absent preclude the analysis of social groups (nationality, religious, or occupational groups) or of factions within the party or state bureaucracies which may have 'nonantagonistic' conflicts of interest relevant to routine foreign policy making.[53]

Area specialists have devoted a great deal of attention to nationality problems in Eastern Europe; in particular, the existence of significant minority ethnic groups is thought to impose constraints on policy implementation. The three official minorities in Romania are Germans, Hungarians and Jews. Experts concur that Ceausescu, like Dej before him, is basically assimilationist. Under Ceausescu, however, there has been a careful effort to ensure the requisite rights (e.g. schooling in one's own language) to avoid political fallout from ethnic dissatisfaction. In foreign policy making the status of the Hungarian minority is most sensitive as it directly affects relations with neighbouring Hungary. The question of Transylvania (is it truly Romanian or Magyar?) is still considered a sensitive issue by the communist leadership. Much historical revisionist effort is employed by linguists, historians and archaeologists to accumulate ever more evidence that the area has 'always' been inhabited by Romanians. The status of Jews, and, more importantly, their right to emigrate has been manipulated by both Dej and Ceausescu to gain economic benefits — economic agreements with Israel and most-favoured nation status from the United States.[54] Overall, it is easy to agree with Jowitt's conclusion that the party retains its directive role. Nationality differences are 'allowed for and even supported rather than intimidated so long as they are individual rather than collective (or structurally expressed) and cultural rather than political'.[55]

Serious evidence of bureaucratic conflict over foreign policy decisions is nearly non-existent in Romanian case studies.[56] There was apparently no significant party faction in the 1970s which could be said to have shared a coherent and opposing interpretation of priorities in opposition to that of Ceausescu. Certainly, individual definitions of national objectives vary, and they can sometimes be correlated with the primary bureaucratic responsibility of the individual in question, especially when budgetary allocations are at issue. An example relevant to the shift in Romanian foreign policy from militant nationalism to selective (economic) cooperation is the removal of Ion Gheorghe Maurer, a key figure in the party's history since the 1930s and Prime Minister from 1961 onwards. Maurer was removed from state office by Ceausescu in 1974 after a controversy in press and public speeches questioning established investment priorities and suggesting the need for technological innovation and increased attention to popular consumption. As head of the Council for Ministers, Maurer had primary responsibility for executing economic policy. In an apparent effort to reduce dissension, Ceausescu restructured the bureaucracy. He created a new Supreme Council of Socio-economic Development in 1972 to coordinate all planning under his personal direction and, after Maurer's dismissal, he gave himself the legal prerogative to chair meetings of the Council of Ministers when the situation warranted.[57]

Efforts to account for the significant reorientation of Romanian foreign policy in 1970-71 by reference to the presence or absence of this or that domestic or external factor do not yield a wholly satisfactory explanation. An approach derived from political economy is more enlightening because it uncovers the structural developments underlying the immediate situation for decision making. The cumulative impact of more than a decade of heavy industrialisation in Romania had by 1970 revealed to the Romanian political élite the limits of semi-autarkic development and thus the necessity for an external policy better able to serve new economic needs. As David Lane rightly argues when he speaks about modernisation and economic development, 'The distinctive feature about . . . state socialism is that the polity plays a much more dominant role in these processes than it does in the more advanced stages of capitalism'.[58]

High rates of investment since 1960, with over 12 per cent annual increases in fixed industrial assets, had established a core industrial infrastructure in Romania but also threatened to exhaust the possibility for further extensive growth (i.e. increasing factor inputs rather than increasing their efficiency). Serious resource shortcomings had emerged by 1970. The shift to intensive development would require imports of advanced technology. Purchase of western machinery, however, had already led to balance of payments difficulties with a one billion dollar hard currency debt accumulated by December 1970. Industrialisation had brought other changes in trade composition, such as a rising deficit in industrial raw materials. Romania was becoming more dependent on imported raw materials while diversification of sources of supply was limited. The Soviet Union still accounted for 70 per cent of Romania's iron ore and 50 per cent of coke (for steel production) in 1970. The disastrous floods in 1969 forced élite awareness of the fragile national resource base.[59] Faced with the consequences of domestic structural changes, the Romanian political élite adapted its foreign policy to economic necessities. It moderated the assertive nationalism and unilateralism in bloc politics (which had suited semi-autarkic development priorities) and in its place elaborated a strategy of selective economic cooperation within both the socialist and the world capitalist economy.

At the level of ideology, the Romanian leadership formalised its new orientation at the National Party Conference in July 1972 where Romania was formally identified as a developing nation — an identity concept which became 'the linchpin of its view of domestic and international relations'.[60] At the level of policy, the new priorities were elaborated at the XI Party Congress in 1974. 'The development of our economy will be achieved under the conditions of an ever more intensive participation in the international division of labour, in commercial exchanges and economic cooperation on a world plane'. To improve Romania's position in the international division of labour and serve national development needs, emphasis was placed on advanced technology, export competitiveness and industrial cooperation.[61] Romania's official status as a less developed country served to justify sacrifices demanded of the population, to rationalise claims for special privileges from Comecon partners and advanced capitalist nations, as well as to promote new forms of cooperation with less developed nations in the third world.

At home, mobilisation of resources to modernise industry and enhance export competitiveness implied relative neglect of consumer needs. Constant defence of this economic policy suggests less than perfect consensus among strategic élites. Ceausescu explained to the National Conference of the Association of Engineers and Technicians that his goal was 'catching up with the developed countries both concerning *per capita* production and the population's living standard. I wish to make it very clear, comrades, that our national income today is about 500 to 600 dollars anually. No matter how we divide those 500 to 600 dollars, even if we spent the entire sum for consumption . . ., we still could not devote to consumption as much as with a national income of 2,400 dollars annually'.[62] Four years later, despite the intervening bureaucratic reorganisation following Prime Minister Maurer's forced retirement over economic issues, propaganda organs persistently reiterated that Romania was engaged in a 'Race Against Time'. 'In the competition for development, the Romanians had and still have to recover a big handicap (sic) . . . it is necessary to further allocate a considerable part of the national income to development, namely some 33 per cent. Any other alternative, whether for the development of the national economy or for raising the welfare of the population is simplistic and flagrantly erroneous . . .'[63]

Romania's acceptance of the Comecon Comprehensive Programme (1971) marked the shift to selective cooperation within the socialist bloc. Peter Marsh documents the interstate bargaining process in which Romania managed to convince its allies to draft a text which 'reaffirmed the commitment of Comecon to equalise economic development levels as a precondition of full integration and adopted word for word the Romanian formula on socialist state regulation'.[64] Using the programme as a touchstone, Romanian élites seek to extract specific benefits from Comecon collaboration:

> In its capacity as a developing country, Romania expects that this cooperation will improve the contribution of the foreign factors to meeting its requirements, such as: . . . investment . . . import of raw materials . . . necessary machinery and equipment . . . modern, highly efficient technologies; expanding foreign markets to sell national products . . .[65]

Joint production ventures with the Soviet Union are now sought if they secure needed industrial inputs. This pragmatism is reflected in statements like the following: 'As a result of its participation . . . Romania will ensure its own long-term supply of natural gas, cellulose, asbestos and ferro-alloys'.[66] Plan coordination with its allies is accepted, but only in specific areas, such as machine tools, where it can create 'prerequisites for a continuous increase in the volume of machinery and equipment exports from the less advanced countries'.[67] At the 29th session of Comecon in 1975, while the USSR introduced Draft Plans for Multilateral Integration, Romania's prime minister sought credits and investments for five Romanian industries and 'access of the industrially less developed socialist states to more advanced technology, to the latest technical and scientific discoveries'.[68]

Given its demands for access to technology and markets for its industrial products in bargaining with the advanced socialist countries, the Romanian leadership readily saw the logic of a shared identity with third world nations. In 1976, the Romanian Central Committee Executive Political Committee announced that Romania had been admitted to membership in UNCTAD 77.[69] New forms of North-South relations are being experimented with — such as joint equity firms to exploit raw materials (for example, KMIL in Kenya and COEMIN in Chile). Promotion of Romanian industrial exports, often facilitated by credits to the third world governments, frees hard currency for importing more advanced western machinery.[70]

The Romanian government also exploits its less developed status in East-West relations. Romania gained special preferences for its exports from the European Common Market on this very basis.[71] At the CSCE Romanian delegates mobilised a coalition of 'European less developed countries' (including Spain, Greece, Yugoslavia and other countries) to militate for exceptions to each general economic principle negotiated. Romania joined both the International Monetary Fund and the World Bank in 1972 and received some 290 million dollars in hard currency loans from the Bank within the first two years of membership.[72] In order to acquire technology, know-how and marketing opportunities from western firms, Romania turned to new forms of industrial cooperation. In addition to licensing, subcontracting, and co-production arrangements, revision of the Romanian legal code (1971) now permits direct foreign private investment on Romanian soil.[73] In East-West, North-South and intra-socialist relations Romania has elaborated a foreign policy of selective cooperation — rationalised by reference to its less developed status — in order to extract economic benefits to serve new domestic development priorities.

The problem of degree

How different is Romania's foreign policy behaviour today compared to that of the other European socialist states? Although a case study of one country may best allow us to understand the motivations shaping policy choices and to appreciate changes over time, only comparison across the universe of similar states, using aggregate data analysis, permits us to establish whether the outcomes are indeed country-specific or of a more general nature. Two examples from the issue-areas of economic cooperation and security may help to place Romania's external behaviour in perspective.

International trade and financial data are excellent indicators for foreign (economic) policy of socialist states. In contrast to advanced capitalist systems, foreign trade remains a state monopoly so that the choice of product, the choice of partner and the mode of financing imports are political decisions. Romanian choices to diversify geographically in favour of Western capitalist partners, to import machinery in particular, and to tolerate trade deficits with recourse to borrowing to cover hard currency needs turn out to be typical and general rather than idiosyncratic when placed in the context of Comecon international economic behaviour.[74] Overall, since 1963 'the share of intra-CMEA (Comecon) trade has been diminishing to roughly 58 per cent of the total foreign trade of the CMEA area in 1973'.[75] From 1961 trade with the western industralised countries, imports in particular, began to grow at a faster annual rate than intra-bloc trade. All Comecon countries have accumulated dramatic hard currency debts due to imports of Western machinery.[76] All Comecon states have moved to experiment with new forms of industrial cooperation with Western firms, as well as with third world governments where the focus since 1970 has been on extracting raw materials in exchange for equipment and technical assistance.[77] Poland and Hungary have also introduced legislation in the 1970s to permit joint equity ventures with capitalist firms. Romanian initiatives on issues of economic cooperation thus no longer appear at variance with the trends toward greater participation in the international division of labour for all the Comecon member states.[78]

As for issues of military security, using aggregate data collections, political scientists tend to make the alliance the unit of analysis and monitor trends in NATO-Warsaw Pact conflict and cooperation by content analysis or events-data analysis.[79] The relative conformity of any one member state thus cannot be determined. In one important arena, however, the Conference on Security and Cooperation in Europe (1973-75), Romanian diplomatic behaviour obviously diverged from that of its allies. In order to examine Romanian negotiating behaviour and test for relative diplomatic autonomy, this writer submitted a formal questionnaire to a stratified sample of twenty Western and non-allied heads of delegation. All informants singled out Romania, and Romania alone, as the one Warsaw Pact country to take an 'independent' position in conference negotiations. Romanian divergence was most pronounced in the issue-area of military security (the CSCE's First Committee) where Romania promoted inclusion of principles on the 'non-use of force' and 'territorial integrity' which often conflicted with announced Soviet preferences. In debates on confidence building measures, such as advance notification of troop manoeuvres, Romania supported proposals tabled by the nonaligned caucus rather than the Warsaw Pact version. Western delegates observed that Romania alone did not always take part in The Warsaw Pact caucus convened before each session to coordinate interventions during the plenary meetings.[80] The complete answer to the question of how different is Romanian foreign policy behaviour from that of other socialist states clearly requires more effort to monitor trends over time and to distinguish between arenas (East-West, Comecon, etc.) and issue areas.

Conclusion

The study of foreign policy making in communist countries is much more exciting when done comparatively. Comparison helps move us beyond description to focus attention on interesting analytic questions. In the Romanian case a small, less developed and supposedly subordinate member of the Soviet regional alliance system initiated an independent foreign policy in 1964. We wanted to know why. Why should Romanian foreign policy prescriptions and practice have diverged from that of other states sharing the same mode of production (state socialism), dominant ideology (Marxism-Leninism) and basic institutional arrangements? Different levels of development, historical experiences, and political culture helped to distinguish the setting for Romania's foreign policy making from that of other similar states. As Arthur Kalleberg succinctly put it, 'Classification is a matter of either/or while comparison is a matter of more or less'.[81] Why did Romania's foreign policy orientation change, at first (in 1966-69) to militant nationalism, and then (after 1970-71) to selective cooperation? Here we identified those changes in the international environment creating opportunities or constraints for the Romanian leadership, as it viewed the world through the prism of its new nationalist version of official Marxist-Leninist ideology. We also discussed those domestic considerations — bureaucratic politics and power consolidation by Ceausescu — which affected the policy making process. One of the major conclusions to be drawn from the study is that after a decade of rapid industrialisation, underlying structural changes obliged the Romanian political élite to recognise that its development priorities were no longer best served by the protective nationalism of the 1960s. Modernisation in the 1970s required selective reintegration within both the socialist and the international division of labour. Socialism, nationalism and underdevelopment have been welded together to forge an ideology to rationalise the new foreign policy of selective cooperation in intra-communist, East-West and North-South relations. In closing, the study suggested that, with better data collections, comparison should enable us to specify just how much Romania's foreign policy outcomes differ from those of other communist countries.

Notes

[1] Although I will refer to 'East European' states or 'socialist' and 'communist countries' for stylistic variety, I define Romania and the other Warsaw Pact members as 'state socialist' systems — a generic term intended to type them by mode of production. They are socialist (as opposed to state capitalist) because neither formal ownership of the main means of production nor effective control over social surplus is in private hands and most importantly, because political and ideological values take precedence over economic efficiency and profit in guiding decisions about production and exchanges. This appelation does not exclude the possibility, which I consider to be actuality, that production relations are exploitative or that a small group, best delimited by those holding party nomenclatura posts, occupies a privileged position in the social division of labour. Whether or not this group should be regarded as a surrogate class — despite the fact that individual members cannot reproduce themselves (heredity); nor directly use social surplus for personal benefit (although indirectly allocative decisions reinforce their basis of bureaucratic power); nor retain privilege once deprived of office — constitutes a fascinating question discussed with special reference to the writing of European Marxists in Alec Nove, 'Is There a Ruling Class in the USSR?' *Soviet Studies* (October 1975). They are 'state' socialist (as opposed to purely socialist) because outside Yugoslavia there have not yet been purposive, concentrated efforts to diminish the role of the state — in accumulation, exchange, legitimation or coercion — in favour of the direct producers.

[2] Two interesting kinds of cross-system comparison will thus be neglected. Diachronic comparison would look at foreign policy making in Romania before 1944 (as a state capitalist system); synchronic comparison could look at non-socialist states which share a particular attribute with Romania such as subordinate status in alliance (Belgian NATO policy) or state-directed industrialisation (Venezuelan technology transfer policy). Romania was compared to other small

European states in my 'Small States and Inter-European Relations' *Journal of Peace Research*, No. 2 (1972). Nicolas Spulber draws both cross-time and cross-system comparison (with third world states) in his book *The State and Economic Development in Eastern Europe* (New York: Random House, 1966).

[3] R. Barry Farrell, *Political Leadership in Eastern Europe and the Soviet Union* (Chicago: Aldine, 1969), p. 89.

[4] James N. Rosenau, 'Pre-theories and Theories of Foreign Policy' in R. Barry Farrell (ed.), *Approaches to Comparative and International Politics* (Evanston: Northwestern University Press, 1966), p. 65.

[5] Richard N. Cooper, *The Economics of Interdependence* (New York: McGraw-Hill, 1968), p. 4.

[6] Ibid.

[7] Stephen Fischer-Galati, however, propounds the thesis that Romania's independent course began much earlier: 'At least as early as 1955 Gheorghiu-Dej and his associates were cautiously pursuing national policies first formulated in 1945 and envisaging a possible eventual assertion of independence from the Kremlin'. See his book *The New Rumania* (Cambridge: MIT Press, 1967), p. vii. For two persuasive refutations questioning Fischer-Galati's data, see Kenneth Jowitt, *Revolutionary Breakthroughs and National Development, The Case of Romania 1944-1965* (Berkeley: University of California Press, 1971) chapter 13 and Jacques Levesque, *Le Conflit sino-sovietique et l'Europe de l'Est* (Montreal: Les presses de l'université de Montréal, 1970), pp. 106-7.

[8] The debate over specialisation in Comecon is nicely summarised in J.M. Montias, *Economic Development in Communist Romania* (Cambridge: MIT Press, 1967), chapter 4,

[9] David Lane, *The Socialist Industrial State; Towards a Political Sociology of State Socialism* (London: George Allen and Unwin Ltd, 1976), p. 15.

[10] Montias (fn. 8).

[11] Statistical data can be found in the appendices to Henry L. Roberts, *Rumania: political problems of an agrarian state* (New Haven: Yale University Press, 1951) and in Ivan T. Berend and Gyorgy Ranki, *Economic Development in East-Central Europe in the 19th and 20th Centuries* (New York: Columbia University Press 1974), p. 308 ff.

[12] Gur Ofer analyses Bulgaria's growth strategy, drawing comparisons to Romania, in 'Effects of Intra-Socialist Trade on Industrial Structure, Growth and Efficiency: A Case for Specialization in Agricultural Goods' 'Jerusalem: Hebrew University/Department of Economics, September 1976).

[13] Berend and Ranki (fn. 11), p. 37.

[14] Berend and Ranki (fn. 11), p. 50, citing E. Niederhauser.

[15] In the debate over industrialisation in the 1960s Montias found RCP elites referring favourably to those interwar bourgeois economists who had promoted import substituting industrialisation as acting in the national interest. Montias (fn. 8) p. 231. The best study of agriculture in twentieth century Romania is

Roberts (fn. 11). Hugh Seton-Watson gives a good picture of Romanian class relations in *Eastern Europe between the Wars, 1918-1941* (Cambridge: Cambridge University Press, 1945).

[16] Hugh Seton-Watson, *The East European Revolution* (New York: Praeger, 1951).

[17] The cost of reparations to different East European states is calculated in Nicholas Spulber, *The Economics of Communist Eastern Europe* (New York: Wiley 1957) and Paul Marer, 'The Political Economy of Soviet Relations with Eastern Europe', in S. Rosen (ed.), *Testing Theories of Economic Imperialism* (New York: D.C. Heath, 1974), pp. 231-60.

[18] Jowitt (fn. 7) p. 249-50. In the discussion which follows, I rely heavily on the only two authors to have carried out comprehensive comparative research on Romanian policy making — Jowitt and Levesque (fn. 7). For a review of their principal arguments see Robert L. Farlow 'Romania: The Analytical Breakthrough', *Newsletter on Comparative Studies of Communism*, VI, 2 (February 1973).

[19] Levesque (fn. 7) p. 261. Levesque may exaggerate the intellectual debt to Russian marxism. See Michael Kitch, 'Constantin Debrogeanu-Gherea and Rumanian Marxism', *The Slavonic and East European Review*, LV, 1 (January 1977), pp. 65-89.

[20] Kenneth Jowitt, 'An Organizational Approach to the Study of Political Culture in Marxist-Leninist Systems', *American Political Science Review*, Vol. 68 (September 1974), p. 1188.

[21] Ibid.

[22] Levesque (fn. 7), pp. 99-101.

[23] Jowitt (fn. 20).

[24] Levesque (fn. 7), p. 140. Support for the Soviet Union in foreign policy was however accompanied by anti-Russian nationalism in domestic politics as Dej's rivals were identified as pro-Moscow, anti-nationalists. See Levesque (fn. 7), p. 133-37 and Fischer-Galati (fn. 7) chapter 4.

[25] Levesque (fn. 7), pp. 162-63,

[26] William E. Griffith, *Sino-Soviet Relations, 1964-1965* (Cambridge: MIT Press, 1967), p. 11.

[27] Levesque (fn. 7), p. 177.

[28] All quotations from the 1964 Declaration, officially entitled 'Statement on the Stand of the Romanian Workers' Party Concerning the Problems of the International Communist and Working-Class Movement' are taken from the complete text as published in Griffith (fn. 26), pp. 269-96.

[29] For an exegesis of this remarkable text see Kenneth Jowitt, 'The Romanian Communist Party and the World Socialist System, a redefinition of unity', *World Politics* (October 1970), pp. 38-60.

[30] Charles W. Kegley, Jr, *A General Empirical Typology of Foreign Policy Behaviour* (Beverly Hills: Sage Publications — International Studies Series,

1973), p. 8. The American invention of events data analysis — monitoring the international press by means of quantitative content analysis — represents an effort to standardise the concept of foreign policy behaviour. For discussion of the promises and perils of this technique see Kegley et al. *International Events and the Comparative Analysis of Foreign policy* (Columbia, S.C.: University of South Carolina Press, 1975).

[31] See Robert L. Farlow, 'Romanian Foreign Policy: a case of partial alignment', *Problems of Communism* Vol. XX (November-December 1971), pp. 54-63 for more detailed analysis of this phase.

[32] Patrick J. McGowan and Howard E. Shapiro, *The Comparative Study of Foreign Policy, a survey of scientific findings* (Beverly-Hills: Sage Publications, 1973), pp. 46-7.

[33] Levesque (fn. 7), p. 236 dates China's disaffection with Romania from Chou En Lai's last visit to Bucharest in June 1966.

[34] The détente diplomacy of the small East European allies is detailed in Jeanne Kirk Laux 'Divergence ou Coalition: la position des pays de l'Europe de l'Est à l'égard de la Conférence sur la securité et la cooperation en Europe 1965-1972', *Etudes internationales*, IV, 1-2 (mars-juin 1973).

[35] Soviet plans to consolidate the Warsaw Pact are discussed in Malcolm Mackintosh, *The Evolution of the Warsaw Pact*, Adelphi Paper, No. 58 (London: IISS, 1969).

[36] The data is available in Laux (fn. 2), pp. 157-58.

[37] Nicolai Ceausescu, *Romania pe drumul desavirsirii constructiei socialiste* (Bucharest: Editura politica, 1968), Vol. I, pp. 412-13.

[38] Romania had undertaken a series of initiatives in UN *fora* after first bringing together nine European small states — selected to represent the WTO, NATO and the nonaligned — to co-sponsor a General Assembly resolution on European cooperation in December 1965,

[39] Ceausescu (fn. 37), Vol. II, p. 416.

[40] Mary Ellen Fischer in, *Ceausescu and the Romanian Political Leadership: A study in the Transfer and Consolidation of Power* (Unpublished PhD dissertation Harvard University, 1974), identifies these three techniques.

[41] A good example of the new integral approach to history is Cornelieu Vasilescu, *Romania in International Life* (Bucharest: Meridiane, 1969). I have documented Ceausescu's use of international issues for building popular support in a comparative study of top leadership Communications in Romania and Poland. In Romania I found a high degree of personalisation — Ceausescu made virtually all public speeches (rather than other Politburo members or appropriate state officials). His focus on foreign affairs issues was heavy (93 per cent of all speeches) and aimed particularly at town meetings (rather than strategic party organisations). Laux, 'Intra-Alliance Politics and European Détente: The case of Poland and Romania', *Studies in Comparative Communism*, VIII, 1-2 (Spring/Summer 1975), pp. 98-122.

73

[42] Ceausescu (fn. 37), Vol. II, p. 567 and Ceausescu, 'The Leading Role of the Party in the Period of Completing Socialist Construction' (Bucharest: Agerpres, May 7, 1967). James F. Brown, 'Romania Today', *Problems of Communism* XVIII, 1 (January-February 1969), gives a good account of Ceausescu's success in removing potential enemies and solidifying his leadership during this period.

[43] See Fischer (fn. 40) and Trond Gilberg, *Modernization in Rumania* (New York: Praeger, 1975), chapter 3.

[44] Ceausescu (fn. 47), Vol. III, p. 415-16.

[45] Serious pressure on Romania to host joint manoeuvres began at the WTO Political Consultative Committee meeting in Budapest in March 1969. During 1969-70 the Albanian and Chinese press sounded the alarm to warn against Soviet intention to invade Romania . . . See *Le Monde* (April 14, 1969) and citations in Robin A. Remington, *The Warsaw Pact* (Cambridge: MIT Press, 1971), pp. 138-53.

[46] Quiescence does not imply subservience. Conflict occasionally erupts dramatically — as when Ceausescu leaked Soviet requests for an extra-territorial corridor through Romania for troop transfers to the international press in 1974. Within Comecon, any efforts to impose political coordination are vigorously challenged. Tentative Comecon-EEC contacts in 1975 provoked Romania to submit a separate document at the 29th Comecon session. 'The Romanian Proposal regarding contacts between Comecon and the EEC' pushed for bilateral governmental contacts and sought to limit Comecon competence to general 'framework' discussions without direct consequence for member states. *Scinteia* (July 5, 1975), p. 5.

[47] James N. Rosenau, 'Comparison as a State of Mind', *Studies in Comparative Communism*, VIII, 1-2 (Spring/Summer 1975), p. 57.

[48] High level Romanian party and military visits to China (1970) were crowned by Ceausescu's visit in 1971. China granted Romania a 200 million dollar interest free loan, agreed to construct three factories and signed its first long term trade accord in a decade with Romania in 1970-71.

[49] In East-West security politics, 1970-72 saw agreement to convene the CSCE preparatory talks in Helsinki and to conduct troop reduction negotiations (MBFR) among interested parties only; signature of the Berlin accord and of the two Germanies treaty.

[50] Kenneth Jowitt, 'Political Innovation in Rumania', *Survey*, 93 (Autumn 1974) describes the 'combined efforts towards hierarchical unification . . . and organizational compression (i.e. through extension of the Socialist Unity Front's control over certain social and cultural organisations) . . .' p. 139-40. Fischer notes one change in technique — rotation rather than promotion of cadres typifies post-consolidation personnel policy. Personal communication from M.E. Fischer. Further material on Ceausescu's leadership can be found in Jowitt, 'Inclusion and Mobilization in European Leninist Regimes', *World Poli-*

tics, XXVIII, 1 (October 1975); in Radio Free Europe reports — e.g. Robert R. King 'Rumania on the Eve of the 11th Party Congress' (Rum/18 November 15, 1974) and 'Ceausescu's Ideological Role is Strengthened' (RAD Background Report/167, July 29, 1976); and in Fischer (fn. 40).

[51] Bill McGrath and Simon McInnes make one of the more intelligent critiques in '"Better Fewer but Better": On Approaches to the Study of Soviet and East European Politics', *Canadian Slavonic Papers*, XVIII, 3 (September 1976).

[52] For a Marxist class analysis of state socialism, see C. Castoriadis, 'Les rapports de production en Russie', in his collected essays, *La société bureaucratique*, vol. I (Paris: Editions 10/18, no. 751 1973) and the references provided by Nove (fn. 1).

[53] As a matter of fact, much of the controversial Skilling collection which purports to identify interest group activity actually deals with what we now call 'Bureaucratic politics' or bargaining among actors within the state (or party) apparatus. H. Gordon Skilling and Franklyn Griffiths (ed.) *Interest Groups in Soviet Politics* (Princeton: Princeton University Press, 1971). The bureaucratic politics paradigm came from Graham Allison, 'Conceptual Models and the Cuban Missile Crisis', *American Political Science Review*, XXIII (September 1969), pp. 689-718.

[54] Joseph Alpern, 'Les relations entre Israel et la Roumanie de la guerre des six jours a la guerre de Kippour (1969-1973), '*Politique étrangère*', No. 6 (1973), pp. 725-52.

[55] Jowitt (fn. 7), p. 282. M.E. Fischer provides a statistical summary after conceptual discussion in 'Nation and Nationality in Romania', Paper presented at the Annual Meeting of the AAASS (Atlanta, Georgia, October 1975).

[56] A model article using the bureaucratic politics paradigm is Jiri Alenta's 'Soviet Decision-making and the Czechoslovak Crisis of 1968', *Studies in Comparative Communism*, VII, 1-2 (Spring/Summer 1975), pp. 147-73.

[57] Radio Free Europe, Rumanian Situation Report 18 (November 14, 1974). Ceausescu also used the technique of bureaucratic restructuring to enhance hierarchical unification in the military-security issue area after General Serb was arrested in December 1971 for passing defence secrets to the Soviet military attaché. A new Law of National Defence gave the State Council (headed by Ceausescu) greater authority over the Ministries of Defence and of Interior. Ibid. and *Le Monde* (Paris), February 16, 1972.

[58] Lane (fn. 9), p. 73.

[59] Detailed analysis of these trends from 1970-75 is provided in J.M. Montias, 'Romania's Foreign Trade; An Overview', pp. 865-85 in 'East European Economies Post-Helsinki', A Compendium of papers presented to the Joint Economic Committee, 95th Congress, 1st Session (Washington: Government Printing Office, 1977. For a comprehensive analysis of Romania's industrialisation strategy, see Marvin R. Jackson, 'Industrialization, Trade, and Mobilization in Romania's Drive for Economic Independence', Ibid, pp. 886-940.

Romania is an oil producing nation but it must import 'iron ore, metallurgical coke, cokable coal, ferroalloys, oil, cellulose, asbestos, nickel, copper, titanium, apatite concentrate, vegetable raw materials' according to N. Belli in *Revista economica*, No. 2 (January 10, 1975) as translated in Radio Free Europe Rumania Press Survey, No. 985 (February 6, 1975).

[60] Jowitt, *Survey*, 1974 (fn. 50), p. 138. Romanian élites likened their dilemma to that of less developed nations well before 1972 — see J.M. Montias, 'Background and Origins of the Rumanian Dispute with Comecon', Soviet Studies, Vol. XVI, 2 (October 1964), pp. 125-51.

[61] Romanian Communist Party, 'Directives of the XI Congress of the Romanian Communist Party concerning the 1976-1980 Five-Year Plan and the Guidelines for the Economic and Social Development of Romania in the 1981-1990 Period', (Bucharest, 1974).

[62] Speech given May 19, 1972, translated by Foreign Broadcast Information Service, *Daily Report*, May 23, 1972.

[63] *Romanian Bulletin* (August 1976), p. 3. Jowitt outlines the tensions stemming from 'the growing heterogeneity of Romanian society (a product of intense economic development)' in Jowitt, *Survey*, 1974 (fn. 50) and the successful efforts to dissipate them in Jowitt, *World Politics*, 1975 (fn. 50). The technical-managerial élite, which many see as posing a special threat to the authority of parties legitimised by reference to the working class and whose senior cadres are accustomed to relying on bureaucratic-dirigiste methods of rule rather than rational criteria, does not appear to be critical to understanding Romanian foreign policy making.

[64] Peter Marsh, 'The Integration Process in Eastern Europe 1968-1975'. *Journal of Common Market Studies*, XIV, 4 (June 1976), p. 325.

[65] N. Belli, 'Equalizing the Economic Development Levels of the Socialist Countries', *Revista Econimica*, No. 13 (September 1974) translated by Radio Free Europe, *Rumania Press Survey*, No.980 (October 390, 1974).

[66] R. Constantinescu, 'The Dialectic of the Rapprochement and Equalization of the Economic Levels of the Socialist Countries', *Era Socialista*, No. 24 (December 1974) translated by Radio Free Europe, Rumania Press Survey, No. 983 (January 22, 1975).

[67] Ibid. Constantinescu proposed a rank of degrees of economic advancement. The USSR is a 'global economic power', followed by East Germany and Czechoslovakia among the 'most advanced countries in Europe', Poland and Hungary at an 'average level of economic development' and finally the 'agricultural-industrial countries' Cuba and Mongolia along with Romania. (Bulgaria is omitted!)

[68] *Scinteia*, July 6, 1975, p. 5.

[69] *Romanian Bulletin* (April 1976).

[70] Radio Free Europe RAD Background Report/180 (December 22, 1975), gives a complete listing of Romanian credits to twenty states (all less developed).

By 1977 Romania had undertaken some 120 industrial cooperation ventures with less developed countries, including 27 joint equity companies, for details see *Revista Economica*, July 15, 1977.

[71] Romania applied for general preferences to the EEC on February 29, 1972. The EEC considered the request but postponed its decision in June 1972. Romania lobbied for support and the French were won over, 'strictly for political reasons', according to *Le Monde* (January 31, 1973), p. 4. The EEC Council of Ministers then agreed in principle in June, 1973 to give Romania preferences effective January 1, 1974. See European Community *Background Note*, No. 13 (August 15, 1974), pp. 6-7.

[72] Radio Free Europe, Rumania Situation Report/5 (February 5, 1975).

[73] N. Manesu, 'Mixed Companies and International Cooperation', *Lumea* (Bucharest), No. 4 (January 18, 1973) summarises Romanian motives and gives references to the pertinent legislation. See C.H. McMillan and D.P. St. Charles, *Joint Ventures In Eastern Europe: a three country comparison* (Montreal: C.D. Howe Research Institute, 1974) for case studies of foreign direct investment.

[74] Montias (fn. 59) documents the trends for Romania.

[75] B. Askanas et al. *Structural Development in CMEA Foreign Trade over the last fifteen years (1960-1974),* Weiner Institut fur Internationale Wirtschaftsvergleiche, Forschungsberichte, No.23 (February 1975), p. 1.

[76] Ibid., Table 6.

[77] On Comecon indebtedness see Lawrence J. Brainard, 'Financing Eastern Europe's Trade Gas', *Euromoney* (January 1976). He calculates that Romania ranked second of the six in terms of the ratio of debt to hard currency export earnings: Bulgaria 2.5; Romania 1.69; Hungary 1.55; Poland 1.26; Czechoslovakia .83; DDR .54. On East-West industrial cooperation patterns see Economic Commission for Europe, *Analytical Report on Industrial Cooperation among ECE Countries* (Geneva: United Nations, 1973). On Comecon relations with the third world, see UNCTAD 'Innovations in the practice of trade and economic cooperation between the socialist countries of Eastern Europe and the developing countries' TD/B 238 (1970).

[78] The USSR relies increasingly on imported technology for key growth sectors with long term pay-back in production preferred. This new orientation can be dated from the ninth five year plan which made imported technology an integral rather than a residual factor in planning. Despite its relative autarky and ideological conservatism (excluding direct foreign investment, for example), the Soviet Union has rapidly extended both its own foreign investment in the west and its foreign banking network. See Philip Hanson, 'The Import of Western Technology' in Archie Brown and Michael Kaser (eds), *The Soviet Union Since the Fall of Khrushchev* (London: Macmillan, 1975/1978, pp. 16-49, for a solid technical evaluation and Herbert E. Meyer, 'This Communist Internationale has a Capitalist Accent', *Fortune* (February 1977), pp. 134-48 for a general description.

[79] For example, Kjell Goldmann, 'East-West Tension in Europe 1946-1970; a conceptual analysis and a quantitative description', *World Politics*, vol. 26, No. 1 (October 1973'. Ole Holsti et al., *Unity and Disintegration in International Alliances: Comparative Studies* (New York: Wiley and Sons, 1973), looks at alliances and attempts to measure national deviations, but China is the selected case.

[80] Jeanne Kirk Laux 'Les négociations Est-Ouest: le role des pays d'Europe de l'Est au sein de la CSCE', *Etudes internationales*, VI, 4 (December 1975) pp. 478-500.

[81] Arthur L. Kalleberg, 'The Logic of Comparison: a methodological note on the comparative study of political systems', *World Politics*, 1 (October 1966), p. 81.

4 Foreign policy making in the German Democratic Republic: the interplay of internal pressures and external dependence

PETER MARSH

Introduction

Although it must be acknowledged that the starting point for the analysis of any Eastern European state's foreign policy is its dependence on the Soviet Union this should not lead political scientists to conclude that this is the only influence on foreign policy making in communist countries. Recent analyses of Soviet and Eastern European domestic politics have cast doubt on the use of the totalitarian model in understanding the political processes of modern industrialised socialist societies; similarly, recent studies of the regional grouping centred on Comecon and the Warsaw Pact have begun to invalidate the 'bloc' concept of Soviet-East European relations. It can thus be said that the 'reconceptualisation' of communist studies, to use Ghita Ionescu's term, has well and truly begun, bringing with it a considerable improvement in our knowledge of domestic and foreign policy making in communist countries.[1] As far as the latter field is concerned, it is now beginning to be realised that the 'dependent' position of the Eastern European states can be, and has been, manipulated by national political élites to defend domestic interests and extract concessions from the Soviet Union. The latter's hold over Eastern Europe has therefore varied in its extent, conditioned by the changing domestic and international forces which have determined the scope for Eastern European independence of action.[2]

However, it is fair to say that on the whole the study of politics and foreign policy making of the German Democratic Republic (GDR) has been bypassed by these changes of approach in communist studies. Indeed, the assumption upon which this study is based, namely that the GDR can 'make' foreign policy, albeit within prescribed limits, would be questioned by many academic observers. For so long considered the archetypal 'satellite state', the GDR has only recently been paid the compliment of serious scholarly investigation into its politics. Even now, however, East Germany remains something of a special case, perhaps one stage further behind the other East European states in the transition from the

79

ghetto of communist politics into the mainstream of political science studies. Only with political recognition, so long the major foreign policy goal of the GDR, has academic recognition at last begun to follow — confirmation perhaps of the East German leadership's faith in the importance of the traditional state system and behavioural political science's touching respect for it.

Of course, the particular nature of the GDR will ensure that, as J.M. Starrels has noted, 'there will always be an argument between those analysts who view the GDR as a unique system . . . and those who see the experiences of this "other German" system as lying within a broader comparative framework'.[3] Starrel's belief that 'perhaps the GDR has finally reached the "take off" stage for students of comparative politics' is based on recent explorations into the political sociology of the GDR — begun by Peter Ludz and taken up by T. Baylis and others — which have at last shed some light on the GDR's political process and the socio-economic factors that influence it. Together, Ludz and Baylis have pioneered a theoretical approach to the study of GDR politics which deserves to be followed by other political scientists anxious to explore this relatively unexplored area of communist studies.

The basis of the work of Ludz and Baylis has been élite theory, and quite naturally it has been assumed that if theories of élite conflict can be found to be useful in the study of Soviet and Eastern European politics they are equally likely to be applicable to the politics of the GDR. In his influential work, *Parteielite im Wandel* (Party Elite in Transition), written in 1969, Ludz argued that industrial development and social change in the GDR had affected a transition from 'totalitarianism' to 'consultative authoritarianism'. As a result of this transition Ludz pointed to a potential struggle for influence on policy making between the traditional stretegic élite (party functionaries, leading cadres) and an institutionalised counter-élite of professional and technocratic elements whose views had increased in importance with the emphasis on economic growth and material welfare in the modern GDR. More recently, in a full-length study of the East German technical intelligentsia, Thomas Baylis expanded on his previous work on GDR politics and attempted to modify Ludz's views. Baylis accepted Ludz's description of the growth in political influence of a new 'technocracy' but contended that its members had been absorbed into the GDR political process as junior partners in power rather than rivals for it. This viewpoint has received further support from a recent sociological study of the GDR by J. Krejci, who argues that Ludz's 'conflict model' of GDR politics is an overstatement when applied to the GDR under Honecker. In Krejci's view, technocratic elements have lost influence under the new leadership, and they affected decision making only in a feedback sense with real power firmly held by the party and state bureaucracies.[4]

Regardless of the different emphasis of the works of Ludz, Baylis, Krejci and others, their common assumption is that GDR politics has been influenced by the socio-economic changes associated with the development of a modern industrial society. What is lacking in this debate, however, is a detailed study of an area of GDR policy making to test the rival theories. It is arguable that GDR foreign policy, and foreign economic policy in particular, is a suitable area for such a test and that the concept of élite conflict is a useful one for understanding the evolution of GDR foreign economic policy in the last decade.

Unfortunately, the traditional assumption that the GDR does no more than play the role of 'little Sir Echo' to the Soviet Union has discouraged researchers from even bothering to test the validity of the generalisation by detailed empirical analysis of East Germany's domestic and foreign policies. The belief that the GDR's relationship with the Soviet Union and East German foreign policy in general has remained static in the face of the growth of the GDR into one of the world's most industrialised societies is at best a gross oversimplification and at worst an excuse for not probing beneath the 'satellite' stereotype. As Wilhelm Bleek has pointed out,

> On a superficial level, the GDR seems to rely more and more on the Soviet Union — if one takes daily proclamations of socialist brotherhood between the two states as signs of dependence. In fact, however, the GDR has a greater influence on the policy formulation of communist parties and other communist states than before and does not shrink from asserting its own interest.[5]

This may be an overstatement of the GDR's current position but it is certainly far preferable to the uncritical acceptance by Western opinion of the GDR's own propaganda line of unswerving devotion to the Soviet Union and complete harmony of interests between the two states. Ironically, the man most responsible for cultivating the image of 'the special relationship GDR-USSR', Walter Ulbricht (the former East German leader), became extremely sensitive to the West's belief in it and was a vociferous champion of the GDR's national identity, even in socialist gatherings. Thus, at the meeting of communist party leaders to discuss the ultimatum to Czechoslovakia in July 1968, Ulbricht was the only leader who tried to insist that the document be sent not just in Russian but in all the other languages of the socialist states. As he reportedly put it,

> I cannot be expected to send an official letter to the Czechoslovak-ian leadership in Russian. This would be more grist to the mill of the imperialists who always claim that I follow Russian not German policies in my country.[6]

The sensitivity of Ulbricht on the question of the GDR's national identity is perhaps the key to an understanding of the social, economic and political dynamics which have influenced East German foreign policy making during the last two decades. The achievement of international recognition and the establishment of a specific national identity have been the primary goals not just of the GDR's foreign policy but of its domestic policy as well. Two major strategies have been employed to attain these goals. They are:

> 1 Close economic and political integration of the GDR with the Soviet Union and the Eastern European states;
> 2 The maximisation of the GDR's industrial strength and the material welfare of its population through the modernisation and further development of the national economy.

It is fair to say that the direction of GDR foreign policy making has been influenced, especially in the last decade, by the interaction of these two strategies and the contradictions that have arisen between them. Thus only a thorough analysis of the GDR's overall political and economic development can provide an understanding of the pressures acting on the foreign policy of the GDR. These pressures have shown themselves most clearly in the sphere of foreign economic policy and relations with the Soviet Union. The following analysis will concentrate on these areas in the period from 1965 to 1976 and will argue that the basic force shaping GDR policy formation has been the conflict between the needs and demands of the GDR as a modern industrial society and its external dependence on the Soviet Union, both factors being crucially important to the achievement of the ultimate goal of domestic and international legitimacy.

Economic change and external constraints

The impact of economic change on East German politics has been well put by Baylis who noted that from 1963, and the introduction of the New Economic System of Planning and Management (NES),

> The record of East German politics . . . is one of continuing conflict, sometimes latent, sometimes overt, between policies justified by the requirements of ideology or politics, and others answering to the demands of economic rationality.[7]

Such a statement could only lead one to expect that, in the field of foreign policy, the GDR's ideological stress on its close alliance with the Soviet Union has not always squared with its attempts to achieve domestic and international legitimacy through the performance of its domestic economy and foreign trade. An analysis of GDR foreign policy in the period from 1965 to 1976 reveals this tension between economic rationality and political necessity, and the isolated outbreak of real conflict between 'strategic' and 'technocratic' elites. The resolution of this conflict and tension, and the restoration of stability to the GDR's external relations, came only in the period from 1971 to 1976 and at the expense of the political career of Walter Ulbricht. The conflicts created by the GDR's foreign economic policy and their contribution to the downfall of the key figure in GDR politics will thus be examined in the course of this analysis.

The early impact of economic reform 1962 to 1965

The majority of studies of East German domestic and foreign policy point to the continuous development of the GDR as a loyal and conservative state very much subject to the dictates of the Soviet Union.[8] If any independent initiative in GDR politics is acknowledged it is described as short-lived and a temporary aberration from the norm of total conformity to Soviet policies. This independent interlude is usually associated with the period from 1962 to 1965 when the introduction of the New Economic System of Planning and Management with its search for economic efficiency (via domestic and foreign economic policies) temporarily put the economic policies of the GDR in conflict with the political necessity of maintaining harmonious relations with the Soviet Union.[9]

For a time Ulbricht himself was carried away by the success of the reforms and declared the period had arrived where 'economics' was taking precedence over 'politics'.[10] He sanctioned the increase in influence of technocratic elements in the GDR, such as economists, managers and technical specialists, at the expense of traditional party functionaries, in the belief that economic modernisation could bring domestic political legitimacy and international recognition more quickly than simple reliance on Soviet backing. The decentralisation policies of the NES and the introduction of elements of the market economy (although extremely moderate by the standards of other Eastern European reforms) had the effort of giving more authority in domestic and foreign economic policy making to technocratic elements who did not share the party officials' automatic loyalty to the Soviet Union and the Eastern European states. Consequently, foreign economic policy was being conducted mainly on the basis of criteria of economic efficiency.

The result was a falling-off in the GDR's economic commitments to the Soviet Union, which the East Germany party leadership (SED) had made a fundamental part of its policy of integration into the Soviet bloc since 1949. Not surprisingly, many party functionaries were alarmed by this tendency of GDR economic interests to be pursued at the expense of political and economic obligations to the Soviet Union and were critical of Ulbricht's enthusiastic backing of the reforms. When the Soviet leadership also began to be worried by the diversion of GDR exports to the West at the expense of the Soviet market, and acted to reverse this trend by political pressures, the traditional party functionaries were able to reassert their authority in GDR politics at the expense of the technocrats; Ulbricht fell in line by accepting an even greater economic and political subservience for the GDR.[12]

From this point of view the conclusion of the Soviet-GDR five year trade agreement in December 1965 is usually seen as the turning point in GDR politics and the end of an independent GDR foreign economic policy. In fact, the suicide of Erich Apel, the chief architect of the GDR's independent economic policies at the time of the agreement, and the re-emergence of the old party functionaries, such as Honecker, launching an attack on 'Westernisers' in the GDR, were evidence of this reversal. The increased trade commitments to the Soviet Union were further proof of the defeat of an independent GDR foreign economic policy. Honecker, in December 1965, seemed to sum up the situation perfectly, and most Western observers concluded that the fragile bloom of GDR independence had died. As Honecker pointed out, the GDR has resumed its traditional foreign economic policy line and was back in the fold. He attacked the trend from 1962-65 quite categorically, stating that

> Some scientists, technicians and civil servants have not yet overcome the tendency to take the 'Western level' as their standard in all questions relating to new technical methods, without having made the effort to discover what the situation is in the Soviet Union. This

is one of the main reasons why the demand for imports from the Western countries continues to increase ... The leaders and all responsible employees in state and economic organs must always start in their practical work from the fact that close collaboration with the USSR is decisive in order to make our long-term prospects secure.[13]

'Close collaboration with the USSR' therefore appeared as the triumphant foreign policy line in December 1965. The GDR was to settle down to its role as loyal supporter of the Soviet Union and orientate its investment and production programme to the supply of the Soviet and Eastern European market.[14] In return for this the GDR hoped to extract greater Soviet and East European support for its campaign for recognition and to increase its influence on the policy making process within Comecon and the Warsaw Pact. Henceforth Ulbricht would become a very vocal supporter of the need for greater political and ideological solidarity amongst the socialist states, especially when new developments such as Bonn's *Ostpolitik* and the Czechoslovak crisis threatened to exacerbate the divisions within Eastern Europe.

Continued tensions 1965 to 1968

Yet it would be a mistake to assume, as many Western observers have done, that 1965 marked the end of the conscious assertion of GDR foreign economic and political interests and a return to complete loyalty to the Soviet Union and ideological orthodoxy. Thus Peter Merkl in a recent study claims to see no evidence of any further élite conflict within the GDR after 1965 and consequently no observable independent GDR foreign policy. He concludes:

there is no evidence that the young counter-élites ever become directly influential in foreign policy-making. To be sure, the temporary attempt of GDR trade in the early sixties to seek a position in the world markets rather than continuing to rely on the Eastern bloc was a major step in the direction of an autonomist foreign policy. But the gallant promoters of this and other reforms appear to have lost their battle for East German autonomy from the Soviet Union[15]

The statement is true in the general sense but fails to realise that the impact of economic reform in the GDR did not subside completely in 1965 but was merely muted by a conscious reassertion of 'politics' over

85

'economics'. In fact, an examination of the GDR's foreign economic and political relations after 1965 reveals that East Germany continued to feel the pull of the NES and its emphasis on economic rationality despite the apparent dominance of considerations of political necessity in its foreign policy. It was only in 1971, with the replacement of Ulbricht by Honecker, that this problem of conflicting interests was really brought under control and the impact of economic reform on the GDR's relations with the Soviet Union effectively neutralised.

In the short term the five-year trade agreement appeared to have checked the dysfunctional aspects of economic reform in the GDR by intensifying the formal obligations of the GDR to the Soviet Union and Comecon. In the years from 1965 to 1970 Ulbricht would use these formal commitments as a basis for intensifying the GDR's political influence in the socialist sphere. From the long term standpoint, however, the increased trade commitments posed an immense strain on the GDR economy because of the pressures to intensify deliveries of advanced manufactured goods and to maintain a favourable trade balance with the Comecon sphere.

In particular, the GDR became concerned to uphold the interests of the advanced industrial states of Comecon against those states who supplied foodstuffs and raw materials. Not surprisingly, this soon led it into conflict with the Soviet Union as the chief producer of raw materials in Comecon and as the major recipient of GDR exports. The growing maturity of the GDR as an industrial state supplying key areas of the Soviet and East European economies thus made it anxious to safeguard the profitability of its intensified trade links. In addition, the continued successful operation of the NES and its partial extension in 1967 to the sphere of foreign trade made it difficult for the Party leadership actually to ensure that the policies of the Vereinigungen Volkseigener Betriebe, or VVB's (the associations of enterprises created by the NES as an intermediate level of economic management), followed the official line of close collaboration with the Soviet Union.

On the surface, GDR foreign policy after 1965 seemed to be a process of intensification of links with the Soviet Union and Eastern Europe for the purpose of making a renewed attempt to increase the GDR's prospects of international recognition. In a report to the Central Committee in December 1965, Ulbricht evaluated the five-year trade agreement primarily in these (political) terms, arguing that it would increase the security of the GDR and strengthen its position in conducting relations with other states, including the capitalist countries. This was the base from which Ulbricht launched an active policy of projecting the GDR on the world scene through contacts with neutral and developing states and, most importantly, of attempting to coordinate the policies of the East European countries on the problem of what sort of economic and political relations should be established with West Germany.

Thus when the coalition government came to power in Bonn in 1966 and began tentative moves for better economic and political relations with Eastern Europe, Ulbricht acted firmly to impose the GDR response on the socialist states as a group. Using the argument that trade was simply a means of splitting the socialist camp, Ulbricht called for increased economic cooperation amongst the socialist states and pointed to the important role that the GDR played in enhancing the total economic strength of the socialist camp.[16] Whilst not afraid to make a virtue out of the necessity of the GDR's increased economic links with the East European states, Ulricht also went one stage further and demanded that such a selfless contribution to socialist solidarity demanded something in return. This was to consist of a guarantee by the other East European states that they would make it a precondition of any official political or economic relations to be established with West Germany that that country first extended diplomatic recognition to the GDR. As one Western commentator put it, this was in effect the creation of a 'Hallstein doctrine in reverse'. Although Romania defied this policy by concluding diplomatic relations with West Germany in January 1967, the policy move was generally successful. Ulbricht secured a further triumph in this respect at the conference of Eastern Europe Communist Parties at Karlovy Vary in the spring of 1967 when all the parties joined in a statement stressing the need to combat West German 'revanchism, militarism and neo-Nazism'[17] and insisted that full international recognition of the GDR, as well as West German acknowledgement of the Munich *Diktat* as null and void *ex ante*, were inalienable preconditions for any 'normalisation' of relations between West Germany and the East European countries.

However, if one were to examine the record of GDR relations with the Soviet Union and its support for economic and political unity more closely it could be seen that throughout the period from 1965 to 1970, when the GDR was building up its image as a strong link in the socialist chain, economic forces were still threatening potential sabotage of the strategy. An analysis of East German foreign economic policy during this period reveals a continued struggle to make the fact fit the theory, and at times produces clear evidence of the latent conflict between the needs and demands of the GDR as a modern industrial state and its deliberately cultivated image as the linchpin of the social state system.

Two issues in particular indicated the GDR's conflicting interests with the Soviet Union — the question of price reform within Comecon and the organisation and composition of foreign trade. As long as the East German leaders continued to believe that their foreign policy goal of international recognition was best served by the strategy of building up closer links with the Soviet Union and the Eastern European states, these issues would be kept in the background. As soon as it became clear that this was not the case, they — and Ulbricht especially — showed a marked lack of the political will necessary to prevent the issues from arousing the hostility of the Soviet Union.

The problem of Comecon price reform, which was raised as early as 1966, remained a touchstone of East Germany's dependence on and subordination to the Soviet Union for the next decade. Initially, when the Soviet Union proposed an increase in Comecon prices for fuel and raw material exports, the GDR joined with Czechoslovakia to champion the interests of the developed industrial states.[18] Almost completely dependent, especially since the 1965 trade agreement, on Soviet raw material supplies, the GDR was concerned to resist Soviet attempts to increase the foreign trade price of raw materials in relation to manufactured goods.[19] As a state committed to the rationalisation of industry, reduction of costs, and the raising of standards to those of the world market, the GDR was extremely reluctant to accept an increase in one of the largest items in its budget. Thus despite its renewed emphasis on loyalty to the Soviet Union a sustained campaign of resistance was launched by GDR spokesmen.

In July 1966 a meeting of Party and government leaders of the Comecon member states in Bucharest failed to agree on a new price policy for Comecon and also rejected the Soviet demand for investment by the Eastern European states in Soviet raw materials extraction and processing. Both prior to this meeting and afterwards GDR economists and other spokesmen engaged in polemics with their Soviet counterparts in the course of which they championed the GDR's case as a modern industrial state whose products were vital to the well-being of all the Comecon countries, including the Soviet Union. In particular, they rejected the idea that manufactured goods were overpriced in relation to raw materials, arguing that a great deal of investment had gone into creating these goods for Comecon's benefit. As one GDR economist told his Comecon colleagues at a special conference on foreign trade in 1967, the supporters of higher raw material prices ought also to include these aspects in their considerations — that there is not only a deficit of raw materials in the socialist world market but also a deficit in high-value manufactured products. . . . Higher raw material prices can thus create the danger of a slowing down in the economic competition with the developed capitalist states, which sometimes, especially in the sphere of science and technology, can be decisive.[20]

Such open criticism of the Soviet position received veiled support from Ulbricht in the economic section of his report to the VII Congress of the SED in 1967. At the Congress he implicitly criticised the Soviet Union when he spoke of difficulties caused to the GDR's industrial competitiveness by costly raw materials and called for foreign trade to be organised on the basis of 'economic criteria'.[21] Clearly, therefore, the GDR was not prepared to accept Soviet demands passively but was determined to put forward its own view of foreign economic relations — a view which at heart was still very much imbued with the spirit of economic rationality stemming from the NES.

A boost was given to this independent viewpoint by the announcement in 1967 of a new stage in the GDR's economic development, leading to what Ulbricht called 'the developed social system of socialism'. One aspect of this new stage was the spreading of the New Economic System into the sphere of the foreign economy, giving greater freedom to the VVBs and Combines (large industrial units independent of the VVB's) to engage in foreign trade on principles of profitability, and transforming the State Foreign Trade Associations into sales organisations of the VVB's rather than retaining them as bodies controlled by the Ministry of Foreign Trade.[22] The aim, according to Ulbricht (who introduced the reform at the Seventh Party Congress), was to bring about 'the confrontation of the enterprise with the conditions of the world market'. He went on to point out how important foreign economic policy was to foreign policy in general and appeared to be arguing that the new reform would help stimulate the GDR's claims for political recognition by establishing the GDR's economic reputation on the 'world market'. This, however, led him to discuss existing foreign trade practice and evaluate its failings.

Ulbricht's assertion, and one which was to lead to a second area of disagreement with the Soviet Union, was that the functions of the foreign trade monopoly of the state, first developed by Lenin as the basis for a socialist state's foreign economic policy, had been misinterpreted in the past. Ulbricht argued that its basic protective function had led to a stifling of initiative and efficiency in the GDR and that the new reforms were intended to remedy this deficiency. This was expressed in his acid remark that 'Our national economy is not a protected reserve for inefficient factories'.[23] However, in the past this *had* been the case because the concept of the foreign trade monopoly — as taken over from the Soviet Union — had been applied too rigidly. In Ulbricht's view: 'It can be stated unequivocably: the foreign trade monopoly has never meant and does not mean now that factories ought not to know or feel the conditions of the world markets'.[24]

The reform of the foreign economic system was to have important effects on relations between the GDR and the Soviet Union because it brought to a head once again the conflict between economic rationality and political necessity which had been implicit in GDR policies since the introduction of the NES. By granting greater potential freedom of decision making to VVBs and Combines, and by putting renewed emphasis on the need to achieve profitability and match world standards of production, the GDR leadership was opening the way to a violation of the harmony between political loyalties and foreign economic policy that it had tried to create since 1965. As Ulbricht tried to tread a delicate balance between two contradictory strategies he found himself increasingly under pressure to make a firm commitment either way. The political instinct which normally told Ulbricht how far he could go was overriden from 1969 by the obsession (stimulated by the prospect of a West German-Soviet détente) that only the GDR was prepared to stand up for itself. Consequently, Ulbricht failed to halt the disintegrative impact of economic developments on the GDR's relationship with the Soviet Union in time to preserve his own political career.

The GDR's decentralisation of foreign trade was only one of a series of foreign trade reforms in Eastern Europe during 1967 which alarmed the Soviet Union. These reforms prompted a series of articles in the official journal *Soviet Foreign Trade* in which Soviet economists warned of the dangers of relaxing the foreign trade monopoly too far, pointing to the difficulties these reforms posed for Soviet exports to the other socialist countries. Soviet concern with the efficiency of its own foreign trade, especially the low percentage of manufactured goods in its exports and the failure to secure price increases for its raw materials, had already been expressed at the highest levels in April 1966. Then Kosygin (in his report to the XXIII CPSU Congress on the five-year plan directives) had stressed the need to increase the export of finished products in order to improve the efficiency and profitability of Soviet foreign trade.

Unfortunately, as Soviet economists now pointed out, the foreign trade reforms in Eastern Europe made it difficult to carry this out.

In particular, the reforms had reduced the effectiveness of the political pressure that the Soviet Union could apply to East European leaderships to make them increase their orders of Soviet goods via the foreign trade sectors of the annual plans. Now decisions about yearly foreign trade were often in the hands of managers and technocrats at lower levels of the administrative hierarchy. As one Soviet economist frankly pointed out with regard to the GDR, Soviet exporters had now no other alternative but to rely on greater efficiency to increase their orders:

> The role of industrial enterprises and their associations in determining equipment imports is being increased [he declared]. In the new conditions, enterprises have a greater incentive to import only modern, highly productive equipment. . . . In this connection, an important condition for further expanding exports of Soviet machinery and equipment to the GDR is improvement of their quality and technical level . . .[25]

There were increasing signs within the GDR from 1967 onwards that managers and specialists within the VVB's and Combines were reluctant to accept Soviet equipment and technical standards. The extension of the economic reform to the foreign trade sphere accentuated the trend towards greater autonomy than before at a time when the GDR leadership was struggling to cultivate close political relations with the Soviet Union and was facing demands in top-level trade negotiations for increased purchases of Soviet manufactured goods and financial contributions to cover the cost of Soviet raw materials extraction. Judging from the exhortations that appeared in the GDR press, namely to recognise the value of Soviet goods and to fulfil Soviet orders, it was evident that the foreign economic reform was beginning to encourage the disintegrative tendencies in GDR-Soviet relations already exhibited in the early 1960s.[26] The crisis in Czechoslovakia (temporarily) halted these tendencies.

The impact of Czechoslovakia on GDR foreign policy (1968-71)

The crisis in Czechoslovakia meant that a premium was being placed on solidarity and the coordination of policies between the Soviet and East European leaderships. It therefore provided Ulbricht with the chance to increase his authority and standing with the Soviet Union by reemphasising the GDR staunch support for the leading role of the Soviet Union on questions of ideology and policy. There was no doubt that Ulbricht genuinely feared the spread of domestic liberalism from Czechoslovakia and was suspicious of the Czechoslovak rapprochement with West Germany. To the SED leadership as a whole, such developments were an anathema, and they had to be stamped out at source before they could infect the populations of other socialist states. It was not difficult to see that Czechoslovakia's economic and social problems were similar to those of the GDR as the other mature industrial economy in Eastern Europe. However, the introduction of *political* — as opposed to *economic* — experiments had no place in the GDR. Domestic liberalism there (in the GDR) would undoubtedly pose a much greater threat to the fragile legitimacy of the regime than in Czechoslovakia. Moreover, the Czech reforms acknowledged the influence of Western social democracy; in contrast, the SED — with one of the strongest Western social democratic parties on its doorstep — quite naturally had no wish to provide any encouragement to such tendencies in East Germany.

Ulbricht's actions after August 1968 thus betrayed how shallow the GDR's outward stance of increasing self-confidence and indifference to West Germany had been in the preceding period. When faced with a potential threat to the political unity of the communist countries, the SED leadership reacted with extreme caution, believing that only in the context of a unified 'socialist state system', based on the principles of 'proletarian internationalism', could the GDR hope to maintain its national legitimacy.[27] Thus, there was no more vigorous advocate of the new conservative line than Ulbricht, who launched a campaign to show the GDR's political and ideological loyalty to the Soviet Union, its rejection of 'market socialism' and its determination to expose the 'splitting tactics' of West German 'imperialism'. Ulbricht now emerged as the spokesman of economic and political orthodoxy backing the Soviet Union's demands for closer economic integration within Comecon, criticising Ota Šik's reformist concepts and warning against excessive dependence on the West through trade.

The recent effects of the NES were an embarrassment to Ulbricht as he posed as the champion of orthodoxy in economic policy. Consequently, a toning down of the pragmatic approach to foreign economic policy of the years prior to 1968 was considered necessary, and a hurried shift was made to bring GDR economic policies in line with the views and demands of the Soviet Union. Ulbricht's pronouncements on economic policy in late 1968 and 1969 were therefore aimed at warning of the dangers of a positive response to West German offers of trade and détente and stressed the advantages of economic and political cooperation among the communist countries. In a speech to the Central Committee Ulbricht even appeared to be advocating a renewed version of autarchy, declaring that 'It is a law of the class competition between socialism and capitalism, that the socialist states must solve each important political, scientific-technical, military, economic or other problem through their own forces'.[28]

However, the reformist influences of recent years could not be removed from GDR foreign policy by a simple change of ideological formulae. Technocratic elements in the decision making centres of the VVBs either failed to perceive the wind of change or deliberately resisted it. Ironically, in the same month when Ulbricht was emphasising the necessity of forging close economic links between communist countries, it fell to Günter Mittag (the foremost 'technocrat' in the party leadership) to scold GDR economic managers and specialists for their failure to appreciate the benefits, including the political ones, inherent in links with the Soviet Union. As he told the Central Committee,

> Unfortunately, dear comrades, and I often have to say this, this clear attitude to cooperation with the Soviet Union and the utilization of the tremendous possibilities resulting from it is still not evident [everywhere]. The main ideological problem that exists in individual enterprises, is the underestimation of the Western threat.[29]

Further evidence that the GDR leadership was moving away from the reformist spirit of the NES in foreign trade matters came in 1969. Despite the publication of an official treatise on the GDR's economic system and foreign trade reforms (which defended GDR experience as being completely in line with Marxist-Leninism, and having nothing in common with 'the revisionist theory of market socialism'), the SED leadership now indicated that it was prepared to pay the Soviet Union's price for continued political security and influence.[30] The Soviet Union at last secured GDR financial participation in the exploitation of Siberian natural gas; a trade protocol, signed in October 1968, announced that Soviet exports of machines and equipment were to increase by 30 per cent; and the draft directives of the GDR five-year plan, published in 1970, projected a 65 per cent increase in GDR trade with the Soviet Union compared to an average of 59 per cent for trade with the other Comecon states.[31].

These concessions to Soviet economic demands were made with the confident expectation of something in return. The 'something' was a greater voice for the GDR in intra-bloc policies and a firm rejection by the Soviet and Eastern European leaderships of Bonn's *Ostpolitik*. The hardline GDR policy on the dangers of West Germany 'revanchism' and 'splitting tactics' was acceptable to the Soviet Union for as long as it was preoccupied with restoring order in Czechoslovakia.[32] The GDR had already firmly articulated its view of Bonn's new policy in 1969 when a prominent ideologist declared: 'When West German government circles speak of their desire for "improvement" of relations between West Germany and the Soviet Union they are always referring to some version of their revenge policy'.[33]

However, when the Soviet leadership changed its policy and decided to respond favourably to the West German initiatives, adopting a strategy of détente, it put an end to the GDR's efforts to set the pace of, and lay down conditions for, improvements in East-West relations. As a result, there was no longer room for the GDR's inflexible stance — nor indeed for the obstinate Ulbricht.

The Soviet Union's determination to improve relations with the Federal Republic, and Poland's active support for the new Soviet policy, were only part of a general upsurge in the desire for intensified contacts with the West. The Soviet-West German Treaty and the Polish-West German Treaty, which were the first fruits of the new policy, symbolised the beginning of a new era in East-West relations that completely altered the GDR leadership's frame of reference. As the altered Soviet viewpoint became clear, and as it emerged that the Soviet Union did not regard West German recognition of the GDR as an inalienable precondition of improvement in relations, Ulbricht reacted indignantly. Despite authorising discussions between GDR and West German representatives on improving relations, his main aim was to try and pressure the Soviet Union into adopting a firmer stance. When it became evident that the Soviet leadership was not prepared to yield, Ulbricht responded with blatant obstructionism, interfering arbitrarily with the flow of traffic from the West to West Berlin and mounting a fierce propaganda campaign against West German claims to hold offical meetings in the city. Thus, as overall East-West relations blossomed under the influence of Soviet detente policy, intra-German relations deteriorated.

By late 1969 and all during 1970 it was becoming very clear that Ulbricht was refusing to bring the GDR in line with the Soviet and East European foreign policy shifts. Inevitably this led him into conflict with the Soviet leaders, and undoubtedly it undermined their faith in Ulbricht's loyalty and political judgement. At first the incidents were minor, such as Ulbricht's use of the 50th anniversary meeting of the Comintern to defend the 1928 view that Social Democracy was the 'main enemy' — a view that had been attacked by Soviet speakers.[34] It was not difficult to draw the implicit parallel to Ulbricht's current attitude to Brandt's SPD and his belief that the East European countries were relaxing their guard. Gradually the rift became more obvious, and Ulbricht spoke out more firmly for what he considered to be the national interests of the GDR.

Thus, in November 1970 — in a speech at an Engels anniversary meeting — Ulbricht dropped all pretence of acknowledging the superiority of the Soviet model of socialism and its formative influence on the GDR. This formula had been standard practice in the GDR. But now Ulbricht pointed to the specifically German nature of GDR socialism which had allegedly evolved by the 'systematic application of the teachings of Marxism in the light of the history of the German workers' movement and the problems experienced in the history of the CPSU'.[35] This relegation of Soviet experience to a subordinate position in the development of the GDR indicated Ulbricht's displeasure with Soviet foreign policy. This displeasure could perhaps have been ignored by the Soviet leadership had it not coincided, whether by accident or by intent, with yet another faltering in economic relations between the two states. Although objective factors, such as the impact of severe weather on industrial production, could be blamed, the decline in GDR exports to the Soviet Union during 1970 no doubt reinforced the Soviet leaders' impatience with Ulbricht. Certainly they no longer regarded him as the loyal and trusted *apparatchik* who always put Moscow first. Having openly challenged the Soviet foreign policy initiatives in 1970, he now appeared either unwilling or unable to halt a deterioration in the GDR's economic commitments to the Soviet Union. The prop of Soviet confidence, on which ultimately Ulbricht had always relied to preserve his domestic political authority, began to be withdrawn as GDR policies appeared to be working against the Soviet Union.

Previously, Ulbricht had always shown an acute awareness of just how important Soviet confidence was to the maintenance of his own domestic authority, even when this meant subordinating his policies to those of Moscow. Thus, in 1953 Ulbricht had reluctantly accepted the 'new course' of economic and political measures proposed by the Soviet leadership in exchange for Soviet military backing against domestic working class discontent. In doing so he had managed to retain Soviet confidence at a time when internal rivals (notably Zaisser and Herrnstadt) were manoeuvering to oust him from power. Similarly, from 1956 to 1958 Ulbricht — taking his line from the Soviet Union, where economic and social reforms were deeply distrusted after the Hungarian and Polish crises of 1956 — had acted firmly to crush the opposition of the economists and managers associated with the views of the reformist economist, Fritz Behrens, and to discredit his leading opponents in the Party Central Committee, notably Schwirdewan, Wollweber, Oelssner and Ziller. On both these occasions Ulbricht moved to align his policies with those of the Soviet Union. At the same time, he was branding the views of his rivals as threats to the stability and orthodoxy of the GDR, even though in the case of the reformist economists and managers he was not averse to adopting some of their proposals (as in 1962-63, when the Soviet attitude to economic reform was less severe). In 1970, however, Ulbricht's acute political sense seemed to desert him, and he could not prevent the Soviet leadership from identifying him with the GDR's failings in foreign economic policy and its obstructionism on the issue of détente. When Ulbricht did attempt to improve his image in Soviet eyes, it was too late: the Soviet leadership had begun to look for an East German leader, who understood correctly the need for GDR policies to fall into line with those of the Soviet Union, and who would carry out the necessary changes.

Some time was still to pass before this would happen. From September 1970 onwards the SED leadership embarked on a campaign to alert the VVB's and Combines to the necessity of fulfilling Soviet export orders in accordance with trade protocols as agreed upon by Soviet and GDR central planners. It was noticeable that Ulbricht did not take an active part in this campaign; it was waged by leading Party functionaries such as Erich Honecker and Paul Verner, both of them members of the SED Politburo. For instance, Verner criticised GDR economic performance in a speech delivered to the Central Committee and promised that 'We pledge ourselves to the Soviet comrades to make increased efforts so as fully to honour our delivery obligations'.[36] This note of firm resolve was taken up in the press, and a general ideological campaign began in 1971, stressing the need to fulfill obligations to the Soviet Union. In January one newspaper emphasised the importance of this trade as follows:

> Some experiences of the past year seem to make it essential for us to remind some enterprises of the need for unqualified maintenance of

delivery standards in punctuality and quality to our Soviet friends. These are no longer trade relations in their old sense, but the fusion of the intellectual and material potentials of our two peoples . . .[37]

Such examples, and they were legion in 1971, testified to the increasing pressure being placed on the GDR by the Soviet Union and the difficulty which the SED leadership was having in translating its policy into action. Inevitably, this difficulty focussed criticism on two areas of GDR life — the leadership itself and the GDR's economic system. From the Soviet Union's point of view, it seemed transparently clear that an improvement in the GDR's export performance could only be made by a recentralisation of control over the organs of production and trade. It was also obvious that Ulbricht, who had derived much of his prestige from the success of NES, and who was behaving intransigently in other areas, did not appear to be capable of carrying out this change. Accordingly, a change of leadership was the first stage in the reorientation of GDR foreign trade policy and foreign policy towards the interests of the Soviet Union. If the Soviet leaders did not take a direct role in Ulbricht's retirement as First Secretary in May 1971, therefore, they certainly did not discourage the domestic opposition in the GDR to assert its power.

Undoubtedly, the changes which took place in East German domestic and foreign policy under the new leadership of Erich Honecker would seem to confirm the view that Ulbricht's retirement was a turning point in the GDR's political development. This turning point however was one which took the GDR full circle, i.e. back to the position of loyal Soviet dependent and model of economic and political orthodoxy, which seemed to be its destiny in the 1950s. But, ironically, this reversion coincided with the achievement of the GDR's major foreign policy aim — recognition by the West as an independent socialist German state.

The return to orthodoxy in GDR foreign policy, 1971-76

Ulbricht's resignation on May 3rd 1971 on the grounds of 'age and ill-health' paved the way for a reassertion of orthodoxy in GDR domestic and foreign policy that was carried out efficiently by the new First Secretatry, Erich Honecker. As a man who had been prominent in 1965 as a critic of the NES's effect on East German relations with the Soviet Union, as a veteran *apparatchik*, and as someone who was not as stubborn as Ulbricht, he was well suited to the task of bringing the GDR into line.

Honecker's appointment was therefore an important move in repairing the damage to GDR-Soviet relations caused by Ulbricht's independent economic and foreign policies.

The reassertion of Soviet influence over GDR politics was in fact to be the key feature of life under the new leadership. This was especially noticeable at the VIII Party Congress, held in June 1971, at which several tendencies in GDR policy under Ulbricht were specifically repudiated. Thus Honecker toned down the praise of GDR developments and reemphasised the importance of the Soviet example, declaring that 'We make the great theoretical and practical experiences of the Soviet Union our own and apply them to our concrete conditions'.[38] What this meant in practical terms was made clear in the final resolutions of the Congress on economic policy which stated:

> In this connection the large wealth of experience of the CPSU and our own experience of the last few years are to be thoroughly evaluated. The running of the economy by the socialist state is to be further consolidated and qualified.[39]

Following the VIII SED Congress a full-scale revision of the GDR's economic and political strategies was carried out which attempted to reemphasise political and ideological considerations at the expense of reformist and technocratic opinion. Honecker announced in late 1971 that 'current economic conditions .... extend the need for central management',[40] and in doing so sounded the death knell for the NES. This attack received rather more crude support from Horst Sindermann (a leading member of the Politburo), who seemed to be accusing the supporters of economic reform of being in league with West German capitalists, arguing that 'During the past two decades there were ample attempts by the West German Monopoly bourgeoisie to restore here, by all counter-revolutionary means, the barbaric principle of profit economy'.[41]

Against such a background of overt propagandising it was obvious that the reformist and pragmatic spirit of NES could not long survive; foreign economic policy would have to be adjusted to meet the new mood of orthodoxy and loyalty to the Soviet Union. In 1972 and 1973 a series of legislative measures recentralised economic decision making quite considerably, and the limited freedom of the VVBs and Combines to determine the direction of their foreign trade was curtailed.[42] In addition new guidelines were laid down for foreign trade that were to result in managers and workers becoming more politically and ideologically aware of their responsibilities.[43]

This reassertion of 'ideological' correctness over 'technocratic' opinion was to be the hallmark of Honecker's version of GDR socialism. Its content consisted of public exhortation to fulfil obligations to the Soviet Union and a nod in the direction of pseudo-workers' power. It was now claimed that the GDR's real strength lay in the hands of its workers, that *they*, rather than the 'experts', were the key to improving production. Needless to say, the emphasis was on working harder rather than being given any greater control over decision making in their enterprises.[44]

With the aid of centralising legislation and a determined propaganda campaign, Honecker succeeded where Ulbricht had failed, the difference in outcome probably being due also to a certain reluctance on Ulbricht's part to curb those forces which had produced the economic growth on which his political prestige had been based. Honecker clearly perceived that Soviet détente policy was likely to transform the international situation and that it was vital for the GDR to have a voice in the settlement of the major problems of European security. This voice would only be listened to if it came from a state that was seen to be acting in a constructive way and friendly to the Soviet Union, both economically and politically. Honecker's policies, therefore, reassured the Soviet Union that the GDR's obstructionism and the 'mistakes' in economic policy had been largely the fault of Ulbricht. On this basis, Honecker could bring the GDR into line with the rest of the East European states behind Soviet foreign policy and attempt to extract some benefits.

The most tangible benefit, of course, was to be a settlement of the German question giving the GDR at least a partial recognition by the Federal Republic. But prior to this, Honecker had been obliged to support a four-Power agreement on the Berlin problem which preserved ultimate control of the access routes to West Berlin in Soviet, not East German, hands. The Berlin Agreement of September 1971 forced the GDR leadership to negotiate with Bonn on the question of transit traffic and visits of relatives, Honecker in the process demonstrating that the GDR was prepared to enter into the new spirit of détente. The Soviet Union responded by exercising some influence on the Federal Republic to move some way towards recognition of the GDR, although it did not make this a precondition of diplomatic relations to be established between the Federal Republic and Poland in September 1972.

The Basic Treaty between the GDR and the Federal republic, signed in November 1972, showed that Honecker realised the importance which the Soviet Union attached to progress on the German question of proof of the sincerity of its détente strategy and proposals for a European security conference. Obviously, this was no time for intransigence, and Honecker was prepared to sign a treaty which allowed both sides the latitude to interpret it according to their own political requirements and prejudices. The Basic Treaty thus authorised an exchange of permanent missions, recognised the separate existence of the two German states in international law and prepared the way for the admission of both states into the United Nations.[45] In the view of the GDR it marked full recognition of the existence of two German states and a defeat for Bonn's policy of claiming to represent the whole of Germany. From Bonn's point of view, the treaty did not abandon the idea of a common German nationhood; it merely confirmed that there were two German states in one German nation.

Honecker had every reason to be satisfied with the prestige that accompanied the Basic Treaty, i.e. the GDR's admission into the United Nations and diplomatic recognition (in two years following the conclusion of the Treaty) by most of the major Western countries. The goal of GDR foreign policy had been achieved by the identification of GDR interests with Soviet détente strategy. If the price was the reimposition of economic orthodoxy and a tightening of ideological control in the domestic sphere then it was a small one to pay for the sense of legitimacy and self-confidence that came with recognition. The Party functionaries could claim that the victory was theirs, based as it was on the GDR's close links with the Soviet Union. The technocrats on the other hand could claim that it was the economic success of the 1960s, stimulated by their reform, which had given the GDR its important position in the Soviet sphere of influence and made its power obvious to the world at large. It was the economic potential which the Soviet Union had thought worth keeping, probably to a greater extent than the ideological and political support which the GDR could offer. The victory of 1972 could thus be claimed to be the product of both strands of GDR foreign policy: (1) loyalty to the Soviet Union and (2) the creation of a modern industrial economy as a nation-building force uniting the population behind the material welfare and security that a *socialist* German state could provide.

What was evident from 1972 onwards was that Honecker was prepared to build on both strategies and consolidate the GDR's position as a modern industrial state firmly anchored to the Soviet Union and the other communist countries. This integrative role played by Honecker was made easier not just by his neutralising the more extreme effects of technocratic reform but also by objective changes in the world economy as a result of which trade with Comecon began to make more sense than the search for 'world-market' participation. In 1973 the onset of the energy crisis in the Western World confirmed just how important a secure supply of fuel and raw materials was to a country like the GDR. Similarly, inflation and depression in the Western countries made trade with them appear an extremely risky business and confirmed the importance of the Soviet Union as a safe market for the GDR's manufactured goods.

Admittedly, the Soviet Union used these changes in the world economy — after several years of having tried in vain — to impose its demands for higher raw materials prices on its Comecon partners, and to secure greater financial investment in the extraction of such materials. But this had to be weighed against the protection which the Comecon trading network provided from the even greater price rises on the world market.[46] The GDR went along with these changes largely because it had little choice. Its basic dependence on the Soviet Union was thus reinforced, although not without a recognition that the new realism in Soviet trade policy meant that fraternal socialist countries would have to pay the price or find an alternative solution to their dilemma. Whether or not the GDR would be able to afford its continued reliance on Soviet energy supplies without the emergence of domestic economic, and perhaps also political, problems remained to be seen.

However, on the political front Honecker's policy undoubtedly paid off, and the GDR once more had Soviet backing for its policy of *Abgrenzung*, or delimitation, pursued with vigour by the SED. The increasing self-confidence of the GDR and its claim to independent nationhood reached a peak at the IX Party Congress in May 1976. At the Congress, Honecker proclaimed the success of the SED's foreign policy, pointing to the fact that the GDR now had diplomatic relations with 121 states. He also declared his opposition to 'revanchist' forces in the Federal Republic who tried to maintain the fiction of one German nation. As Honecker stated quite categorically, 'The GDR will continue to rebut all attempts by reactionary and revanchist forces in the FRG [West Germany] which cling to the thesis — as outdated as it is futile — of keeping the German question open. This question, comrades, is no longer open'.[47] The reason for this assertion that the German problem no longer existed was not just that the Basic Treaty had been signed. It was, according to Honecker, because the GDR was a 'socialist German nation' which embodied all the progressive elements of German history and culture in its national life — a life that was completely different from that of the Federal Republic. This view was reinforced after the Congress by Werner Lambertz, a Politburo member, who spelt out the dissociation of the two German states as follows:

> The independent development of the two socially-opposite German states has continued and they are more closely integrated in the two opposite world systems. ... The basis, content and forms of national life in the GDR have undergone qualitative changes.[48]

The period from 1971 to 1976 had thus seen the complete identification of the GDR with the international communist system not just in ideological and political terms but also in domestic and foreign economic policy. The five-year plan for 1976-80 envisaged a 30 per cent increase in exports to the communist countries and the expenditure of 7,000 million marks on joint raw materials projects with these countries but primarily the USSR. It seemed at last that the demands of economic rationality and political necessity had been harmonised in the GDR's foreign relations and that henceforth there would be none of the disintegrative behaviour associated with foreign economic policy during the Ulbricht period.

However, three clouds remained on the horizon: first, doubts about the ability of the GDR to pay the price for Soviet energy supplies without endangering economic growth; secondly, the ability of the Soviet Union to satisfy the rising demands of all the Comecon countries; and, thirdly, the GDR's continued need for advanced technology to aid the rationalisation of industry — a need that tends to reduce the GDR's consumption of high-cost raw materials. The source of this advanced technology is the West, but to pay for it the GDR has to increase its export of goods in order to gain currency. Until recently, the GDR leadership refused to acknowledge these difficulties. However, in May 1976 the SED launched a five-year campaign to wipe out wasteful use of raw materials and to increase productivity in GDR industry.[50] Following this, renewed calls were made to increase profitable exports to the West in order to pay for advanced Western machinery imports whose costs were soaring due to inflation. Even Honecker, in 1977, was forced to admit that the GDR was beginning to feel the impact of 'capitalism's crisis' and that there had to be a compensatory increase in exports to the West.[51]

Observers of GDR politics could be forgiven for feeling that there was an uncomfortable air of *déjà-vu* about this state of affairs. The question remained whether or not Honecker could balance the conflicting pressures on GDR policy from both East and West and maintain the GDR's increased economic and political loyalty to the Soviet Union. As the new

Treaty of Friendship, Cooperation and Mutual Assistance between the two countries was being signed in 1975, and Honecker (at the Party Congress) was praising 'the indestructable fraternal alliance' with the Soviet Union, it appeared that economic troubles were brewing for the GDR which might test the sincerity of those commitments. Certainly, the GDR's foreign relations looked stable, and its loyalty to the Soviet Union had never been more consciously asserted in foreign policy statements, but the doubts lingered as to how far these links would remain unaffected by economic changes. The past record of GDR politics, and of its foreign relations in particular, had not provided much evidence for excessive confidence in the GDR's ability as a society to live up to the model rule thrust upon it by the SED leadership. Ulbricht had learnt this lesson to his cost, and it remained to be seen whether Honecker could profit from that experience.

Conclusions

The central argument of this analysis is that, no matter how much effort is devoted to domestic sources, GDR foreign policy in the last fifteen years cannot be understood without reference to the overall political and economic relationships of the GDR with the Soviet Union and Eastern Europe. If the fundamental goal of East German foreign policy has been diplomatic recognition, both by the Federal Republic and by the world at large, then the methods of achieving it had been to build up the GDR into a modern industrial economy and to integrate it economically and politically into the international communist system. Unfortunately, the strategy of industrial modernisation has not always complemented the strategy of political and economic integration. The conflict has been most clearly expressed in the field of foreign economic policy where the differences at the domestic level between traditional Party functionaries and elements of the new 'technocracy', associated with the NES, have come to the surface. They have manifested themselves particularly in a conflict over the *objectives* of foreign economic policy, i.e. whether such policy should simply be guided by considerations of political necessity, or whether it should respond to the dictates of economic rationality, regardless of the effect this might have on political alliances and commitments.

For a small state such as the GDR a divergence between its ideological and political commitments and its foreign economic policy has been a luxury it could ill afford. For a time Ulbricht believe that it was possible to let the reformers and technocrats have their way in the hope that their ideas would boost domestic economic efficiency and increase the material welfare and satisfaction of the population. He believed that this could be done without damaging the GDR's main guarantee of existence and security — its relationship with the Soviet Union. What he did not realise was that the technocratic and reformist elements within the GDR might influence the course of foreign economic policy beyond the limits of what was politically safe. When Ulbricht tried to restrain this tendency he found himself in increasing difficulties because he also had identified himself with the economic success of the reforms and had begun to reflect the prestige they had brought to the GDR in his own conduct towards the Soviet Union, including on matters which affected the GDR's security. Ulbricht's fall therefore was intimately connected with the emergence of an autonomous East German identity stimulated by economic success and by transgressing limits acceptable to the Soviet Union.

Indeed, the conflict between the interests of the GDR and the Soviet Union stemmed from this basic divergence between foreign policy and foreign economic policy in the GDR which Honecker sought to remedy. Ulbricht had made clear the importance of foreign economic policy in 1967 when he stated:

Foreign economic relations are one of the basic props of our foreign policy. They have great importance for the internal development of the GDR as well as for its international position and its authority in the world. Foreign policy and foreign economic relations are thus permanently associated with one another and in their practical accomplishment are closely connected.[52]

The growth of economic reform sentiments in the GDR and the emergence of a technocratic element in the Party and state hierarchies, which for a time enjoyed Ulbricht's patronage, removed GDR foreign economic policy temporarily from this firm grounding in political necessity and made it more responsive to considerations of economic rationality. As respect for technocratic opinion within the GDR grew in direct relation to the increasing success of the East German economy in the 1960s, traditional Party cadres found themselves having to relinquish some of the centralised powers of decision making. At times this development produced conflict between 'strategic' and 'counter élites', in Ludz's terms, and created considerable tension within GDR politics, which ensured that there wuld be firm backing for Honecker's attempts to reimpose central control and ideological orthodoxy after 1971. It was not that the Party cadres — who found their spokesman in Honecker, with his well-established opposition to 'Westernisers' — seriously feared a takeover of their power by the new technocratic forces, but that they were reluctant even to consider sharing that power. Consequently, Ulbricht's ambivalent attitude, from 1969 onwards, to the impact of technocratic reform on the East German economy and its effect on relations with the Soviet Union convinced many Party veterans that their old leader was perhaps no longer the best protector of their influence and power.

Once Ulbricht had lost the confidence of Moscow, therefore, there was no shortage of support for his replacement by Honecker as the man who would regain Soviet support and keep technocratic elements firmly in their place. Thus Baylis's notion of an orderly absorption of the new technocracy into a position of 'junior partner' in power is perhaps an overstatement. The disputes over domestic and foreign economic policy in the years from 1965 to 1971 stemmed from a conflict of viewpoint that was too deep to be easily accommodated by the East German political process. Only the political crisis of 1969 to 1971, the fall of Ulbricht, and his replacement by Honecker, could determine the nature of the relationship between 'strategic' and 'technocratic' élites. This process was far from orderly and partly confirmed Ludz's suggestion that élite conflict has played a major role in GDR politics. Certainly, it would be true to say that if the technocracy did finally achieve a 'partnership in power', then the conflicts over domestic and foreign economic policy in the 1960s were part of the process whereby the political élite won the battle to decide on whose terms such a partnership should be based. It is against this wider background of domestic conflict, therefore, that East German foreign policy making should be understood.

As a result of these developments, upon close examination, the GDR did not, behave in the period from 1963 to 1971, like a 'satellite state', as it is frequently characterised. Its behaviour reflected the complex interplay of domestic and international pressures, the most obvious of which were those of economic reform, limited national legitimacy, and the demands of the Soviet Union. Within circumscribed limits it put forward a specific GDR policy line on vital matters — a line that reflected the influence of domestic interests and was not afraid to resist Soviet demands for changes in Comecon prices, central control of foreign trade and other matters of direct concern to East German economic and political interests.

In the last resort the GDR could only go so far in the assertion of an independent foreign policy stance before running up against the basic fact of its political dependence on the Soviet Union. This dependence was intensified after 1972 with the impact of the energy crisis and the Western economic depression on the small communist countries, which virtually put an end to the freedom of manoeuvre characteristic of the 1960s. Nevertheless, when the GDR had the chance to defend its specific economic and political interests it took that chance. An interpretation of East German foreign policy from 1949 to the present as one consistent development towards the role of most trusted supporter of the Soviet Union would be grossly simplistic. Like the rest of the Eastern European states, the GDR responded to the economic and political changes of the 1960s by developing its own national identity. The fact that this development did not go as far as in some states, or lead to dramatic confrontation with the Soviet Union (as in the case of Czechoslovakia), should not be allowed to obscure it. The GDR's foreign policy, particularly on economic matters, was not a carbon copy of the Soviet Union's but it represented the specific national interests of the GDR limited by external constraints. Within those limitations, the case for assuming the existence of a specifically East German foreign policy during the years from 1963 to 1971 can definitely be made and is worth making as a contribution to understanding the complexities of Soviet-East European relations.

Notes

[1] For a good summary of the new approaches to communist politics see G. Ionescu, *Comparative Communist Politics* (London: Macmillan, 1972), pp. 24-35, and F. Fleron, *Communist Studies and the Social Sciences* (Chicago: Rand McNally, 1969).

[2] I have discussed this changing relationship and the forces affecting it in 'The Integration Process of Eastern Europe: 1968-75', *Journal of Common Market Studies*, XIV, 4 (June 1976), pp. 311-35. For recent theoretical treatments of Soviet-East European relations see W. Zimmerman, 'Hierarchical Regional Systems and the Politics of System Boundaries', *International Organisation*, XXVI, 1 (1972), pp. 18-37; K. Kaiser, 'The Interaction of Regional Subsystems', *World Politics*, XXI, 1 (October 1968), pp. 84-108; and N. Jangotch, Jr, 'Alliance Management in Eastern Europe: the new type of International Relations',

World Politics, XXVII, 3 (April 1975), pp. 405-30.

[3] J.M. Starrels, 'Comparative and Elite Politics', *World Politics*, XXIX, 1 (October 1976), pp. 130-42. Starrels is the joint author of one of the most recent works on the GDR; J. Starrels and A. Mallinckrodt, *Politics in the German Democratic Republic* (New York: Praeger, 1975). Another good general work recently published on the GDR is K. Sontheimer and W. Bleek, *The Government and Politics of East Germany* (London: Hutchinson, 1975). Both works attempt to consider the GDR in the light of current political science research.

[4] The works in question are P.C. Ludz, *Parteielite im Wandel* (Cologne: Westdeutscher Verlag, 1969), later published in English as *The Changing Party Elite in East Germany* (Cambridge: Mass: M.I.T. Press, 1972); T. Baylis, *The Technical Intelligentsia and the East German* (Berkeley and Los Angeles: University of California Press, 1974); and J. Krejci, *Social Elite Structure in a Divided Germany* (London: Croom Helm, 1976), p. 105.

[5] W. Bleek, 'From Cold War to Ostpolitik: Two Germanies in Search of Separate Identities', *World Politics* XXIX, 1 (October 1976), pp. 114-30.

[6] This is according to Gomulka's former interpreter, Erwin Weit, who was present at the meetinga: E. Weit, *Eyewitness: The Autobiography of Gomulka's Interpreter* (London: Andre Deutsch, 1973), p. 214.

[7] T. Baylis, 'The New Economic System: The Role of the Technocrats in the GDR', *Survey*, No. 61 (October 1966), pp. 139-53.

[8] The economic and political integration of the GDR into the Soviet bloc as a deliberate policy from 1949 has been well shown by H. Kohler, *Economic Integration in the Soviet Bloc with an East German Case Study*. See also the account of Sontheimer and Bleek, who argue that 1961 and the building of the Berlin Wall gave the GDR the chance to build up its own identity distinct from the Soviet Union — Sontheimer and Bleek, op. cit.

[9] The growth of a more self-confident and independent mood in GDR politics in this period has been noted by many Western observers. See for example; Welles Hangen, *The Muted Revolution* (London: Gollancz, 1966), pp. 42-5; David Childs, *East Germany* (London: Benn, 1969), p. 251; Walter Osten, *Die Aussenpolitik der DDR* (Opladen: Leske Verlag, 1969), p. 64.

[10] Ulbricht asserted this line in a speech to an SED Conference in 1962 — 'Neues Deutschland', 15 September 1962. When the New Economic System was introduced in July 1963, Ulbricht also pointed out the importance of a strong economy in winning international respect and recognition for the GDR. See his speech, 'Strong Economy: Successful Foreign Policy', 10 July 1963, in W. Ulbricht, '*Zum Okonomishchen System des Sozialismus in der Deutschen Demokratischen Republic*'. (Berlin: Dietz Verlag, 1969), p. 238.

[11] I. Spittman, 'The Soviet Union and the GDR' *Survey*, No. 61 (October 1966), pp. 165-77.

[12] Spittman estimates that the share of Comecon countries in GDR trade fell from 75 to 72.4 per cent whilst that of capitalist states (excluding the Federal

Republic) rose from 12.5 per cent to 14.2 per cent. GDR exports were as follows (*in millions of dollars.*)

Year	USSR	Developed capitalist states
1963	1276.5	482.1
1964	1383.6	549.3
1965	1310.6	634.5
1966	1276.5	649.5

Source: P. Marer, *Soviet and East European Foreign Trade, 1946-69* (Bloomington: Indiana University Press, 1972).

[13] Erich Honecker in *Neues Deutschland*, 16 December 1965.

[14] Under the December trade agreement, 56 per cent of the exports of the GDR's electronics industry, 54 per cent of the products of the shipbuilding industry were to go to the Soviet Union. W. Osten, *Die Aussenpolitik der DDR, op. cit.*, pp. 63-4. The Soviet Foreign Trade Minister claimed that the GDR would deliver annually almost one third of the Soviet Union's purchases of machinery and equipment — *Berliner Zeitung*, 4 December 1965. For a detailed account of the qualitative change in GDR trade with the Soviet Union and Comecon from 1965 see K. Pritzel, *Die Wirtschaftsintegration Mitteldeutschlands* (Cologne: Verlag Wissenschaft und Politik, 1969), p. 118.

[15] P. Merkl, *German Foreign Policies, West and East* (Santa Barbara: ABC-Clio, 1974), p. 206.

[16] Between 1966 and 1968, the GDR pursued an active foreign economic policy designed to strengthen its links with the East European states and discourage them from developing economic links with the Federal Republic. This policy was aimed particularly at Poland and Czechoslovakia who were natural trading partners of the GDR in terms of size and proximity and industrial structure. Thus, in these three years GDR trade with the smaller socialist states increased faster than trade with the Soviet Union and the Federal Republic. This policy fitted in with both the GDR's desire for more efficient foreign trade and its concern to increase the unity and common interests of the socialist states against West German initiatives.

[17] M. Croan, 'After Ulbricht: The End of an Era', *Survey*, XVII, 2 (1971), pp. 74-98.

[18] The debate started in Comecon in 1966 and concerned the question of whether or not the existing price system (based on an average of world market prices over the preceding five years) should be changed because it was penalising raw materials producers whose prices reflected the low level of world market prices despite considerable costs of extraction and processing. The Soviet Union won some support for its demands from Rumania and Bulgaria who both felt they were having to pay high prices for Comecon manufactured goods without adequate reward for their own primary exports. Needless to say the GDR, Czechoslovakia, and also Poland and Hungary, as the major producers of manufactured goods preferred to retain the existing system. For details see K. Pritzel, op.

cit., pp. 114-8 and P. Marsh, 'The Politics of Economic Integration in Eastern Europe with Special Reference to East Germany', M.A. thesis, Manchester University 1973, pp. 83-7.

[19] Under the 1965 agreement the Soviet Union was to supply 95 per cent of the GDR's petroleum 66 per cent of its coal, 92 per cent of its timber, 93 per cent of its iron ore, 82 per cent of its rolled steel, over the period to 1970 — *Deutsche Aussenpolitik*, No. 10 (1968), as quoted in W. Osten op. cit., pp. 63-4.

[20] E. Taeschner, 'Die Bedeutung der natürlichen Bedingungen für die Internationale Arbeitsteilung', in *Aussenwirtschaft und Wachstum*, Vol. III of *Theoretische Probleme des Ökonomischen Wachstum im Sozialismus und Kapitalismus*, Proceedings of a Conference held in Berlin 1967 (Berlin: Akademie Verlag, 1968). Other GDR economists at this conference took issue with the Soviet economists I. Dudinski and O. Bogomolov, who had argued that raw materials producers were getting the worst of the bargain in intra-Comecon trade. See especially the contribution by G. Kohnlmey, 'Bemühungen zur Theorie der komparativen Vorteile im Aussenhandel', pp. 95-7. The Soviet viewpoint was put most clearly some time earlier in I. Dudinski, 'The Fuel and Raw Materials Problem of the Countries of the CMEA and Ways to Solve It', *Voprosy Ekonomiki*, No. 4 (May 1966). For a summary of the Soviet viewpoint see P. Marsh, 'The Politics of Economic Integration', op. cit., p. 85.

[21] W. Ulbricht, Report to the 7th Congress of the SED Berlin, 17 April 1967.

[22] For a detailed discussion of the foreign trade reforms see P. Marsh, 'The Politics of Economic Integration in Eastern Europe', op.cit., pp. 97-103.

[23] W. Ulbricht, Report to the 7th Congress of the SED, *Collected Speeches*, Vol. 2, op. cit., pp. 313-4.

[24] Ibid, p. 318.

[25] N. Popov, 'Second Stage of the Economic Reform and the Foreign Trade of the GDR', *Soviet Foreign Trade*, No. 7 (1968), pp. 11-13.

[26] Thus in late 1967, the SED weekly *Einheit* contained a critical report on the import of data processing machinery by certain factories, from West Germany and the USA. It charged 'young university and college graduates' with ignoring Soviet experience in this field and the quality of Soviet equipment, stating, 'From a political and class point of view, the USA and West Germany both attempt to hinder the construction of socialism in the GDR', *Einheit*, No. 12 (1967), p. 1497 f.

[27] Thus although there was some substance to the GDR's fears, the overreaction on Ulbricht's part spoke volumes about the GDR leadership's lack of confidence when faced with sudden external change. As Peter Bender points out, 'Only a feeling of insecurity at home, whether justified or not, causes developments outside the GDR which would strike a well-established regime merely as irritations, to seem dangerous'. P. Bender, *East Europe in Search of Security* (London: Chatto and Windus, 1972), p. 23. W. Zimmerman makes a similar

point when he argues that, after 1968, the GDR alarmed by the 'loosening of the boundaries of the regional system' achieved by Czechoslovakia, acted with Poland to pressure the 'regional hegemon' into 'solidifying the boundaries' so that it might once again feel secure. W. Zimmermann, 'Hierarchical Regional Systems', op. cit., pp. 18-37.

[28] W. Ulbricht, Report to the Ninth Session of the SED Central Committee, *Neues Deutschland*, 25 October 1968.

[29] G. Mittag, Speech to the 9th Session of the SED Central Committee.

[30] The treatise was prepared by a team of authors under the supervision of Gunther Mittag and was intended to set out the official SED view of economic policy. The work was entitled *Politische Ökonomie des Sozialismus und ihre Anwendung in der DDR* (Berlin: Dietz Verlag, 1969). It was withdrawn from publication after Ulbricht's retirement in 1971.

[31] For details see *Soviet Foreign Trade* No. 1 (1969), pp. 13-17 and *Die Wirtschaft*, 5 November 1970.

[32] Melvin Croan has commented on the increasing self-confidence of Ulbricht from 1968 to 1969 and notes that an article in *The New York Times*, 18 November 1968, entitled 'The New Ulbricht Wins a Key Role in the Soviet Block', received favourable mention in *Neues Deutschland*, 6 December 1968; Croan, op.cit., pp. 74-98.

[33] H. Barth, as quoted by P. Bender, *East Europe in Search of Security*, op. cit., pp. 28-9.

[34] The meeting took place in Moscow in 1969; for details see M. Croan, op. cit., pp. 74-98. Another incident which could have been indicative of Ulbricht's displeasure with the new foreign policy line was his failure to attend the Hungarian Party Congress in November 1970. Although Ulbricht excused himself on the grounds of ill-health, the sending of F. Ebert, a minor Politburo figure, as leader of the GDR delegation looked like a deliberate snub to the Soviet and East European leaderships. See *GDR Press Agency*, 13 November 1970.

[35] W. Ulbricht, Speech at the Scientific Conference Commemorating Engels, Berlin, 12 November 1970. *GDR Press Agency*, 13 November 1970.

[36] P. Verner, Report to the 14th Session of the SED Central Committee, *GDR Press Agency*, 9 December 1970.

[37] *Berliner Zeitung*, 13 January 1971.

[38] Erich Honecker, Report to the 8th Congress of the SED, 15 June 1971, *Neues Deutschland*, 17 June 1971.

[39] Final resolutions of the 8th Congress of the SED, *GDR Press Agency*, 21 June 1971. Numerous statements substantiating this change in GDR policy and affirming the value of the GDR's relations with the Soviet Union appeared in the GDR press in 1971. Kurt Hager, a prominent Party ideologist for example referred to the strengthening of relations with the Soviet Union as 'a matter of life and death' in a speech to the Karl Marx High School, Berlin, *GDR Press Agency*, 14 October, 1971.

[40] Speech to SED Central Committee meeting, 17 December 1971.

[41] H. Sindermann, Speech on GDR's 22nd Anniversary GDR Radio 6th October 1971. Transcript in BBC Summary of World Broadcasts (Eastern Europe), 9 October 1971.

[42] For details see P. Marsh, 'Politics of Economic Integration', op. cit., pp. 120-2 and M. Keren, 'The New Economic System in the GDR: An Obituary', *Soviet Studies*, XXIV, 4 (April 1973), pp. 554-87.

[43] A clear statement of the new approach to foreign economic policy was presented in D. Albrecht, 'Die Grundlagen und Aufgaben der Aussenwirtschaft nach dem VIII Parteitag', *Sozialistische Aussenwirtschaft*, Nos. 7-8, 1971, p. 1 f.

[44] The new emphasis on working class participation in economic policy and its fulfilment was spelt out in Honecker's 'Report to the 9th Session of the SED Central Committee'.

[45] 'Treaty on the Bases of Relations between the German Democratic Republic and the Federal Republic of Germany'. 8 November 1972, GDR Version, and P. Merkl, op. cit., p. 162.

[46] For the background to these changes as they affected Soviet-East European relations generally, see P. Marsh, 'The Integration Process in Eastern Europe 1968-1975'. *Journal of Common Market Studies* (Vol. XIV No. 4) June 1976, op. cit., pp. 327-33.

[47] Report to the 9th Congress of the SED May 18th 1976 — *Keesings Contemporary Archives*, 6 August 1976, pp. 27875-76.

[48] W. Lambertz, 'New Stage in the Development of the GDR', *World Marxist Review*, Vol. 19, No. 7, pp. 4-7.

[49] Between 1966 and 1970, GDR energy consumption grew by 4 per cent and currently is growing at about 3.8 per cent per annum. The Soviet Union supplies about 80 per cent of GDR crude oil requirements and the price rises have hit the GDR heavily. In addition the Soviet Union is now faced with the problem of setting priorities for its deliveries as supplies decrease and domestic demand rises. Faced with the desire to satisfy home consumption, Eastern European demand, and sell oil to the West in order to earn foreign currency, the Soviet Union has some difficult decisions to take after 1980 when demand will begin to outstrip supply. For an excellent treatment of this important subject see J. Russell, *Energy as a Factor in Soviet Foreign Policy* (Westmead: Saxon House, 1976).

[50] *The Times* (London), 24 February 1977.

[51] *The Guardian* (Manchester), 21 May 1977.

[52] W. Ulbricht, Report to the 7th Congress of the SED, 17 April 1967 in 'Zum Okonomischen System des Sozializmus . . .', Vol. II, op. cit., p. 193.

5 Ideology, organisation and environment: sources of Chinese foreign policy making

ROBERT BOARDMAN

Bracketing China with the Soviet Union and other communist countries in Europe poses a certain irony. The grouping would not commend itself to a Chinese analyst. 'China is a socialist country, and a developing country as well,' Teng Hsiao-ping told the Sixth Special Session of the United Nations General Assembly in 1974. 'China belongs to the Third World. . . . China is not a superpower, nor will she ever seek to be one'.[1] Unease with the alliance of 1950, compounded by older resentments, culminated in the Ussuri River clashes between Soviet and Chinese forces in 1969. In the 1970s perceptions of the Soviet threat have directed and constrained Chinese policies in the Third World, and towards the United States and Western Europe. Following the death of Mao Tse-tung in 1976, the declared willingness of 'the Brezhnev clique' to improve Soviet-Chinese relations was dismissed as so much hot air by Peking.[2] Its own championing of just causes was contrasted by China with both the connivance and the rivalry between Moscow and Washington: both capitalist, both imperialist, each given to nuclear brandishing, neither capable of refraining from interfering in the internal affairs of other states.[3] Despite their mutual antagonism, however, and the profound differences between the Chinese and the Soviet political systems, a working assumption of this contribution will be that the two can usefully be twinned as a device for raising by one rung of generality observations that may be made separately about the foreign policies of each.

This has to be done with some care. But comparison has special value in the case of China. Studies of it, like the country itself, have often given the impression of being isolated. Developments in political science and international relations, or even tendencies in research into other communist societies, have passed by relatively unnoticed. And while changes are evident in our approaches to the study of Chinese domestic politics, these have been rarer in relation to Chinese foreign policy. Research receptors have tended to be open exclusively to information from China, and closed to comparative evidence. Lacking this corrective, studies have been shaped by a kind of amplifying feedback process that has discouraged change. Scholarship has nonetheless been diverse. China is such a vast, complex and varied country, its history so long and the whisper of the past in the present so intriguing, its apparent impermeability to probing by inquisitive foreigners so daunting, its strategic importance for both the United States and the Soviet Union so central, and the record of Western understanding of it so impregnated with myth,[4] that we should perhaps not be surprised to find Western analysts of Chinese foreign policy divided on questions of substance and method. Filing into neat boxes has plagued treatments of Chinese foreign policy probably more so than those of any other major power. 'Soviet satellite', 'Third World revolutionary activist', 'pragmatic moderniser', 'totalitarian party state', 'budding nuclear power', 'inheritor of Chinese tradition' — each image could be elaborated, qualified and justified as a bench mark for interpreting the course of China's relations with other states.

In this chapter, three broad sources of Chinese foreign policy will be examined. The first section, on ideology, treats a number of questions. How do Chinese foreign policy decision makers see the world? To what extent are Chinese world views dependent upon Marxist-Leninist doctrine? Secondly, a section on organisation and foreign policy investigates the character of the decision making process in China. Does the appearance of foreign policy being determined by a relatively small leadership group tally with reality? The question is approached by examining the variety of state, party, military and other factors which arguably can have some influence over the policy process. A third section looks at the impact of China's external environment, regional and global, on its foreign policy. To preface these three main sections of the paper, however, we turn first to some general factors which can be held to condition China's external behaviour.

Chinese foreign policy: explanations from geography, history and economics

Geographical attributes have frequently been suggested as part of the explanation of Chinese foreign policy. Like the Soviet Union, modern China has grown in size, taking in ethnic minorities in the process, from polities having their roots in relatively small regions of what now constitutes the national territory. Differences of terrain, climate and economic organisation remain pronounced as between different parts of the country. There is a classic divide between north and south, overlaced by cul-

113

ture and language; and another between the east and a sparsely populated, non-Chinese west. Internal communications and transportation problems over a land area of 9,561,000 square kilometres inhibit economic centralism. Links with the distant border provinces were poor until well into the 1950s; the opening of new rail connections is still a major event.[5] Regional disparities have posed major policy issues for Peking.[6] As in the Cultural Revolution, political conflicts may erupt between different centres of power. Some of the most strategically sensitive areas, notably Sinkiang and Manchuria, lie outside traditional Chinese definitions of 'China proper', and are particularly vulnerable. The Soviet Union lies along the northern and north-western border, large tracts of which are assumed to be indefensible in the last resort in Chinese defence planning, with the Mongolian People's Republic biting a large half-moon from its middle. One Chinese province, Taiwan, houses the rival Nationalist government. Other territory, lost to China in the nineteenth century, has been a sporadic irritant or source of embarrassment.[7] Its size alone would make China an important focal point of world politics; its location in relation to the Soviet Union, Japan, and the United States gives it a crucial significance in the workings of the Asian international subsystem. In sum, both the given and the changeable elements of Chinese geography have been intimately related since 1949 to the Chinese Communist Party's goals of national integration, territorial integrity, economic development and national security.

Sensitivity to external threat, and concern for international status, may also be a product of the relative newness of Chinese foreign policy. Imperial China had at times flourishing contacts with western Asia. Missions were sent to Africa during the Ming dynasty. But traditional distinctions between the Middle Kingdom, its tributaries, and the barbarians of the world's perimeters, could make no room during the seventeenth and eighteenth centuries for the notions of sovereignty and statecraft then emerging in Europe. A rudimentary foreign affairs machinery appeared in the following century in response to European pressures. National weakness and continued foreign encroachments, however, meant that China was, like Poland or Turkey, more acted upon than actor. Between 1911 and 1949, China was immersed in the drawn out revolutionary process which culminated in the formation of the People's Republic. This dearth of foreign involvments on the part of the Chinese made speculation about the new China's orientation to the rest of the world a hazardous operation. In the terms of the Western policy debate on recognition in 1949-50, were the Chinese Communists on balance relatively more 'Chinese' or more 'Communist'?[8] Did Communist portrayals of the nature of the international system betray a more deeply embedded Sinocentrism?[9] Were later policies towards Korea or Vietnam shaped by memories of their former status in relation to imperial China? Did the Maoist strategy of exploiting contradictions between imperialists originate in more traditional Chinese tactics of playing off one barbarian against another? Is revolutionary rhetoric aimed at Third World countries simply a revised version of a Sinic cultural *mission civilatrice*? More fancifully, can Chinese denunciations of United States-Soviet arms limitation talks be linked to Chinese appreciation during the late Ming period of the dangers of a proliferation to the Chinese population and to others outside the country of firearms and explosives and their technology?[10] Such questions are ultimately unanswerable. Yet the ways in which the past is structured, whether in factional conflict[11] or in assessments of the motives of foreign governments,[12] clearly play some role in the policy process of China.

The state of the Chinese economy can impose harsh constraints on the capacity of the Chinese to implement some goals. Economic factors, indeed, in the form of the imperatives of flood control, have been put forward as a key to understanding Chinese political history.[13] The checks and opportunities set by harvests have been argued to be a determinant of foreign policy initiatives and reversals.[14] More modestly, it is fair to say that the problems of initiating effective, politically acceptable, and ideologically legitimate development strategies in a country with a limited resource base and a population that is approaching the one billion mark,[15] are bound to have implications for foreign policy, and especially if it is accepted that the scope for manoeuvre by Chinese economic planners is markedly less than is implied in totalitarian models of the Chinese system. There are economic limits to the degree to which China can exploit foreign aid as a tool of foreign policy, or speed up the development and deployment of a second-strike nuclear force, or engage in a modernisation programme with minimum foreign help. Such constraints may set limits even to the amount of Chinese attention to and interest in external events, beyond the most pressing questions of national security, or the tailoring of diplomacy to development needs. Chinese appreciations of the military imbalance between the two countries accounts for a large measure of China's Soviet and Soviet-related policy. Economic explanations of this order, though, also leave a lot out of the picture. Tangible support for foreign revolution, for example, has been more contingent upon ideologically self-imposed restraints, assessments of political and diplomatic costs, and the risk taking propensities of particular individuals or groups involved in the policy process.[16]

Ideology and foreign policy

Chinese leaders have from time to time made important statements encapsulating world conditions and trends. This was a game at which Mao Tse-tung for a long time showed unmatched stylistic and analytical prowess, as well as the political skill of timing such interventions so that the attendant prescription carried maximum weight. His argument of June 1949, in *On the People's Democratic Dictatorship*, that 'all Chinese without exception must lean either to the side of imperialism or to the side of socialism', and his denial of the existence of a 'third road', is a prime example of a delicate balance within the Party being tipped in this way.[17] Four years earlier, at the Party's Seventh National Congress, he noted, 'three major contradictions in the old world . . .: first, the contradiction between the proletariat and the bourgeoisie in the imperialist countries; second, the contradiction between the various imperialist powers; and third, the contradiction between the colonial and semi-colonial countries and the imperialist metropolitan countries.'[18] In 1964, Chinese statements refined the notion of the 'Intermediate Zone' first used by Mao in 1946. The 'first intermediate zone' was held to consist of the 'independent countries and those striving for independence in Asia, Africa and Latin America'; the second of 'the whole of Western Europe, Oceania, Canada, and other capitalist countries' which, because 'subjected to US control, interference and bullying', had 'something in common with the socialist countries and the peoples of various countries.'[19] Lin Piao, in a famous essay of 1965, cast world politics in the mould of the Chinese civil war. 'Taking the entire globe, if North America and Western Europe can be called "the cities of the world", then Asia, Africa and Latin America constitute "the rural areas of the world". . . . In a sense, the contemporary world revolution also presents a picture of the encirclement of cities by the rural areas.'[20] In the mid-1970s, change was a recurrent theme, with repeated reference to the 'great disorder under heaven' that characterised world politics, and the 'wind sweeping through the tower [that] heralds a rising storm in the mountains'.

What do such statements tell us about Chinese foreign policy? The view that the ideology of the political leadership of a communist society determines foreign policy goals is unsatisfactory because it is too simple:

116

other factors, including history and geography, have to be considered. Similarly, ideology seen as part of a rational continuum of thought and action, as in traditional Marxist epistemology, errs in assuming that the logic of mental processes can be matched by that of policy processes.[21] The more general question of the relation between ideology and politics in China, however, raises issues far beyond the scope of this chapter. Debate on the nature and influence of Maoism has sustained heated academic exchanges.[22] Chalmers Johnson has observed, nonetheless, that 'one of the most persistent problems, even failings, in the scholarly study of Communist societies has been a simplistic treatment of the influence of ideology on those societies'.[23] The discussion here will look at three kinds of ways in which the relationship between ideology and foreign policy can be approached in the case of China.

Firstly, ideology, in Robert Dahl's sense as 'a set of more or less persistent, integrated doctrines' espoused by the leaders of a political system,[24] can be viewed as functional. Ideology, that is, legitimises leadership roles and translates power into authority. In pre-revolutionary societies, it may justify both rebellion and the roles of rebel leaders, while calling into question the legitimacy of existing political élites. It cannot usually be implanted coercively: a certain resonance with the unarticulated sentiments of a population, founded on culture or circumstance, is required. In terms of political psychology, it may thus meet important cognitive, emotive and social needs of individuals; in terms of political sociology, it may be a crucial cementing factor in the formation and cohesion of political communities. In terms of foreign policy, therefore, an ideology may be argued to be functional for authoritarian or for totalitarian governments to the degree that it can lend credence to real or invented foreign enemies, the threat of intervention from whom can rally peoples around leaders.

The imputed need of Chinese élites to legitimise their power by fostering myths of enemies within and without recurred in Western interpretations of events in the 1950s and 1960s. The appearance of a tough line from Peking suggested that economic failures were needing to be hidden, intra-élite bickering squashed, unrest diverted, or energies channelled. It is interesting to see the same kind of hypotheses reappearing in Soviet analyses in the 1970s, particularly as an explanation of Peking's continued hostility towards Moscow.[25] Two conflicting interpretations are possible. Firstly, the magnifying of foreign enemies, for example the United States, could be seen as serving entirely domestic mobilising functions. It meant that China, preoccupied with her own affairs, would tend to avoid, if possible, foreign entanglements. But secondly, the Chinese could be viewed as being predisposed to welcome, and if possible trigger, tensions on their borders or further afield because of the functional value to them of imperialism. In a study of Chinese political culture, Richard Solomon has noted that periods of major institutional change in China have also been times of war or of the threat of foreign intervention. The first periods of land redistribution by pre-1949 Communist authorities took place during the War of Resistance against Japan and the continuing civil conflict with the Nationalists; land reform was promoted during the final phase of the civil war and completed during the Korean War; socialisation of industry and commerce proceeded in the context of the patriotic movement to 'Resist America and Aid Korea'; communisation was carried out during the Taiwan Straits crisis of 1958; the Cultural Revolution took place during the war in Vietnam and Sino-Soviet border tension. He concludes that

> the tension of a violent confrontation is a context which [the Party leaders] have learned to use to further their social and political goals ... we would observe that a political or military confrontation with an enemy provides the Party with the most appropriate context for promoting the natural translation of anxiety about conflict with a powerful authority into aggressive emotions and legitimised struggle.[26]

He adds, however, that with the exception of the 1958 Taiwan Straits crisis and the Sino-Soviet clashes, the situations of external threat which accompanied, and may have precipitated, major internal change were largely beyond Chinese control.[27]

In the Soviet case, moreover, the proposition that China may have postponed lasting accommodation at some point after the 1969 clashes, or rebutted Soviet moves following Mao's death in 1976, for domestic purposes, is weakened by the high security, economic and political costs of the confrontation to the Chinese, by evidence, including that of high level foreign visitors, that public declarations are congruent with genuine fears, and by other factors, including bureaucratic inertia, the routinisation of defensive preparations, and the obligation of Chairman Hua to demonstrate the continuity of his foreign policy line with that of Mao, which together make for immobility on the Chinese side. In the case of the 1958 crisis, Melvin Gurtov has concluded, after reviewing various Western explanations of Chinese policy, that 'what [they] have in common is their assumption that Mao, whether for primarily domestic or for

118

foreign policy reasons, "needed" an external adventure to make a point'; in his view, alternative explanations of tension in the Straits are more satisfactory and more plausible.[28] Again, other evidence suggests that in practice the Chinese strive to keep separate foreign policy and the heat of domestic politics. During the Cultural Revolution, Western business-men in China were given assurances that China's problems were domes-tic and should not be construed as having consequences for its foreign trade policy. Commitments to continuity in foreign policy were repeated during the later campaign against Lin Piao and Confucius.[29] This is not to deny, though, that there have been unintended consequences for foreign policy of domestically targeted propaganda attacks on other states. These were significant factors exacerbating first American and later Soviet alarm about Chinese intentions, and had implications in turn for the shaping of Chinese policies. And scepticism regarding the enemy-searching hypothesis does not preclude the possibility that such options may have been advocated by some individuals or groups as part of the complex process of policy formation that lies behind China's behaviour.

Secondly, ideology can be viewed as a relatively cheap instrument of foreign policy, where other tools of statecraft may be economically, polit-ically or strategically more costly. For example, it may be held to cloak weakness; deter enemies by instilling in them a myth of the irrationality of the supposed victim; serve to strengthen the mettle of rebels in foreign revolutionary wars; or add bargaining leverage in trade-off situations. The taking by the Chinese of ostensibly perverse stands on some issues for reasons of doctrinal imperative has been accounted for by some obser-vers by reference to this instrumental use of ideology. A number of well publicised statements in the 1960s, drawing chiefly on Mao's writings on the nature of guerrilla warfare, elaborated the theme that 'the atomic bomb is a paper tiger', reaffirmed the supremacy of men over *matériel*, and envisaged post-nuclear war futures safe for China and for socialism. Ambivalence towards this more 'purist' attitude concerning weaponry is present in the late 1970s in moves to set the armed forces on a more securely modernised footing. Resort to ideology, then, may have been part of a defensive strategy in which a hint of irrationality and conse-quently of imperviousness to nuclear blackmail acted as a surrogate for the large gap in weapons systems existing between those of China and those of either the United States or the Soviet Union.[30] Similarly, scen-arios of further Sino-Soviet hostilities in which Soviet land forces are trapped in a protracted anti-guerrilla war on Chinese territory may have been designed by Chinese strategists to tip the balance of argument away from invasion on the part of military circles in Moscow closely familiar with the United States' experience in Vietnam. Gregory Clark, for example, has noted that China was initially motivated to stage the confrontation with the Soviet Union in ideological terms, firstly, because this is how Khrushchev, through the concept of peaceful coexistence, was criticising the Chinese; secondly, because of the traditional role of ideology in debating leadership changes in communist societies, the Chinese perhaps seeing the possibility of adding decisive weight to those leaders in Moscow anxious to oust the Soviet party chief; and thirdly, because the dispute came to involve a search for allies in the communist world in which both sides needed to discredit the ideology, and claims to leadership, of the other.[31]

However, the Chinese strategic calculus, and the image of it which Peking chooses to project to domestic or foreign audiences, cannot be contrasted too sharply. Statements up to a point can be taken as echoing beliefs. This brings us to the third view: the positing of a direct causal link between ideology and foreign policy. Treatment of this relationship in the general foreign policy literature has had a chequered history. Some approaches have seen ideology as a disposable epicarp, and have given greater importance to power configurations in the international system. Others have put emphasis on the significance of cognitions, particularly those of members of decision-making élites, and have sought to identify the part played by ideology in structuring these. Both perspectives have value for the study of China.

Discrepancies between words and deeds in Chinese foreign policy lend weight to the first view. If ideology can mask a policy based upon *Realpolitik* in relation to the Soviet Union and the United States, it can also give way before the demands of expediency. Peking's tolerance of the position of Hongkong for reasons of economic self interest, intelligence gathering, or timidity, provides meat for a stock Russian taunt. The Hsinhua News Agency was still pounding away fiercely at the 'debauchery of the financial magnates and aristocracy' of Britain at a time of good official relations immediately prior to the signing of the 1972 agreement to exchange ambassadors.[32] But it is in relation to the Third World that the issue comes to a head. Rhetorical support for revolutionary change has gone hand in hand with constant repetition of the principle of self reliance. 'The question of world revolution is one thing for the countries concerned', Ch'en Yi declared in 1963.

If countries are not ripe for revolution, then China can't do anything about it. ... China is not the archcriminal behind every uprising. China cannot pour revolutions on or off when she wants to. China can only manage her own affairs. Revolutions depend on the people themselves. But China will support foreign revolutions both morally and politically. We are Marxists. We must support them . . . But it must be noted, Chinese troops will not cross our borders to advance revolution.[33]

A number of important points and qualifications are expressed here, including definitions of the ripeness of countries for revolution, and of the meaning of moral and political support. China's record in Africa suggests some receptiveness to feedback. Chinese officials were expelled from Cameroun in 1961 for allegedly aiding rebel forces, from the Congo in 1964, and from Burundi and Kenya in 1965.[34] Policies in the following decade tended to be more prudent, specific, discriminating and task oriented, for example in the construction of the rail link between Tanzania and Zambia. But with the combined intensification in the late 1970s of both Sino-Soviet tension and of pressures in southern Africa, the job of isolating the sources of Chinese policy has become more exacting. On the one hand, competition with the Soviet Union for political support has become more determined. It would presumably be pursued in the absence of *any* push from ideology, and may even merge into a longer term defensive strategy aimed at preventing Soviet utilisation of land based facilities in Africa in the event of future war between Russia and China.[35] On the other hand, to the extent that Chinese support for liberation forces has had an ideological base, the ideology in question might better be classed with the diffuse socialisms of Africa than the Marxisms of Europe. There has been a comparably uneasy blending of ideological and strategic concerns in other parts of the world, for example in the Middle East and Latin America.[36] Asia, however, has consistently enjoyed a far higher priority for China for reasons of national self interest and security. The ideological component of Chinese behaviour has been perhaps correspondingly lower. C.P. Fitzgerald has described Chinese policy towards the Overseas Chinese as hesitant, indecisive, timid and inconclusive.[37] Responses to the Vietnam war tended to be cautious. In general, approaches to other states in the region have reflected goals related to stable interstate relations, border security, and counter-Soviet posturing, rather than to ideological penetration.[38] During the late 1970s, for example, the Chinese adopted an attitude of encouraging benevolence towards the anti-communist states meeting within the ASEAN (Association of South-east Asian Nations) framework.

Arguments about ideology, however, often have an inconclusive quality that has led research off in other directions. It crops up in a more disguised fashion in studies of Chinese élite perceptions or in related group models of the Chinese policy process. Ideology, for example, may impose an obligation to justify or rationalise proposed foreign policy options. While this could be argued to be a *post hoc* exercise which, given the pliability of doctrinal exegetics, involves minimal constraint, anticipation of such a need may well serve to eliminate some options at an early stage and help promote others. The proven ability of China to implement major policy reversals, as has occurred in relation to India, the United States and the Soviet Union, and to defend these shifts in Marxist-Leninist terms, is not necessarily symptomatic of pragmatism, indifferentism or caprice: foreign policy lines have considerable medium term robustness. And explanations of inconsistencies between declaratory statements and actions can be sought within other conceptual frameworks than power politics; competition between different groups or bureaucracies in Peking is but one example. A large body of research has now been done on the question of just how members of Chinese foreign policy decision making élites see the world around them. Some findings have been based on the amount of attention different media give to various categories of foreign news.[39] Daniel Tretiak focused on the changing percentages of space taken up in the *Peking Review* with discussions of the international environment in general, and of particular countries or regions, to investigate the proposition that China in the immediate aftermath of the Cultural Revolution might be in the process of 'turning out.'[40] Attitudinal studies using content analysis and other methods have been used as adjuncts of group research, for example in studies of the influence of the People's Liberation Army,[41] or of factionalism within the Foreign Ministry and Party Central Committee.[42] There have been a number of related studies of Chinese attitudes towards the Soviet Union[43] and the United States.[44]

The merits of looking at Chinese foreign policy making in this way stand out clearly. Data from publications is readily available in large quantities, even if on specific points these sources may not always be satisfactory. Secondly, such materials, used with care, can give useful pointers to shifts in thinking within the Chinese leadership on particular questions. Thirdly, arenas of competition and conflict between different groups in the policy process can be identified, and the implications for policy explored. The results of such researches tend to support the contention that policy making in China is a complex process, and that we cannot confidently rely on one publication — whether the *Peking Review* or even the *People's Daily* — to give a reliable indication of thinking on policy isues, since we are dealing not with a monolithic but rather with some form of a multi-actor system. This point will be taken up in the next section. On the other hand, a number of interpretive difficulties continue to delay progress on this front. Chinese analyses may be, indeed usually are, voiced with a view to certain effects and with an eye to certain audiences, whether domestic or external. They may, for example, be instrumental in power struggles between contending individuals or factions, and fail, consequently, to expose the 'true' beliefs of decision makers. Further, flimsiness of content in documentation detracts from the vigour with which inferences about attitudes can be made. And more important channels of communication between Chinese officials are generally inaccessible to western observers.[45] Some studies have accordingly laid emphasis more on observable Chinese behaviour, rather than on strategic or theoretical writings, as a guide to the nature of Chinese foreign policy.[46] This does not mean that we should irrevocably sweep away investigation of attitudes. Broader comparative studies of élite perceptions, spanning western as well as developing and Communist societies, would seem to hold most promise for the future.

Organisation and foreign policy

The ideological commitment of Party members has both structured Chinese politics and institutions and been itself shaped by them. The Chinese system, though, has not evolved in ways comparable to that of the Soviet Union. Still less has it fitted neatly into the variety of totalitarian models devised primarily to account for developments in the European context. More particularly, (1) administrative and economic centralism falls foul of Chinese realities; (2) organisational forms have in general not been such as to augument the freedom of manoeuvre of foreign policy elites; (3) it is not clear that any one man, or any small group, has consistently forged policy; and (4) it is not certain that the governmental foreign affairs machinery has been subject to overall strategies of political guidance from the Party that constrain, supervise and direct its day to day activity. Policy processes may be obscured, rather than prised open, by a study of institutions. The Chinese have a predilection for leaving high offices vacant, as occurred with that of the Foreign Minister in the years following the Cultural Revolution, and for multiple role-filling at senior levels embracing state, party and military bodies. The convening of meetings of Party and governmental organs has been irregular. Informality and even experimentation have left their marks on decision making. Maoist distrust of the dehumanising and deradicalising effects of bureaucracy has given institutions a susceptibility to the ebb and flow of politics that differentiates them from those of the Soviet Union.[47]

Both theoretical and practical problems impede study of the foreign policy process in China. Dissastisfaction on the part of Western analysts with totalitarian models has left a vacuum only inadequately filled by pluralist, group or conflict alternatives. Insights explored in relation to Western systems, such as the bureaucratic politics model, cannot automatically be translated into a communist context. The generally secondary status of government bureaucracies, including foreign ministries, *vis-à-vis* Party bodies, the imbuing of Party members in governmental organs with the principles of democratic centralism, and the role ideology can play in erecting common goals, set stringent limits to theories or models positing more horizontal or competive patterns of interaction between groups. We will turn later to the central question of how relations between actors in the foreign policy process are structured in China.

Secondly, more practically, communist states take a good few stages further the problems of access confronting students of Western systems. 'The Chinese Communists', Franz Schurmann has written, 'have created the most powerful government in Chinese history, but extreme secrecy about its operation makes it impossible for us to study it in detail'.[48] Two kinds of circumventing strategies have been deployed. Firstly, attention can be concentrated afresh on ideology. Robert North has argued that 'Chinese foreign-policy making, at least, is still highly centralized. The ideas of the men at the top, therefore, assume primary importance in explaining policy. And these ideas are available to us, as detailed analyses of institutions and processes are not'.[49] Harold Hinton, secondly, has argued that the problem of secrecy is 'less serious than it might appear. The policy-making process itself, for practical purposes, can be "black-boxed"; in other words, we not only cannot know for sure but do not really need to know what actually goes on inside the leadership at such times, since we know the outputs (policies) from foreign as well as chinese sources and since, especially with the advantage of hindsight, we can form a fairly clear idea of the inputs (the objective situation, perceptions, considerations, and so forth) that contributed to determining the shape of the policy in question'.[50]

These escape routes notwithstanding — and issue can be taken with the assumptions behind each — a great deal of often painstaking effort has now been invested in attempts to see with greater clarity the interstices of the Chinese foreign policy process. We can look first at the more easily identifiable institutional actors, and then at ways of conceptualising and analysing the process itself.

The formal Party institutions can be summarised quickly.[51] The National Party Congress has met at irregular intervals since the Seventh Congress of 1945. Central Committee plenums elect the leadership of the Party and debate and ratify policy changes. In between plenums, power rests with the Politburo, and in particular with its Standing Committee. This simple picture, however, hides a reality of considerable complexity. While the National Party Congress is properly the final authority and source of legitimacy of Party policy, and despite its role in confirming Central Committee membership changes, the lengthy periods between its successive convenings and its cumbersome character as a decision making forum have persuaded observers to focus instead on Central Committee plenary sessions and the Politburo. Plenums enjoyed particular authority in the late 1950s and early 1960s. Foreign affairs, though, have rarely been central to their agenda. Schurmann's summary of the sixteen between 1949-62 suggests an overwhelming priority to internal affairs.[52] Major shifts of policy can, some commentators have argued, be traced to some of the plenums. Simmonds, for example, has identified three of them over this same period in which foreign policy orientations were defined within a broader setting of national goals. The Third Plenum of the Seventh Central Committee, held in June 1950, affirmed the Party's emphasis on reliance on Soviet support following the treaty of the previous February, and a stand of implacable opposition to the United States; the Seventh Plenum of August-September 1956 questioned the acceptability of continued dependence on Soviet material aid; the Tenth Plenum of the Eighth Central Committee of September 1962 inaugurated a phase comprising severe strain in Party and state relations with the Soviet Union, the war with India, and later the 1964 nuclear test.[53]

The lens of such formal meetings is clouded, however, by the holding of extraordinary meetings consisting of some or all Central Committee members, and their uncertain relationship with the variety of Politburo-centred fora that have emerged in China. The Standing Committee of the Politburo was usually identified, before the Cultural Revolution at least, as the crucial foreign policy making group, the decisions of which filtered hierarchically down through party and government machinery. Its importance in the decade before 1966, indeed, can be seen from the prestige and personal authority of its members: Mao Tse-tung, Liu Shao-ch'i, Chou En-lai, Chu Teh, Ch'en Yun, Lin Piao, and Teng Hsiao-ping. But, as Donald Klein has pointed out, what truth there is likely to be in this assumption is difficult to verify because of a paucity of supporting evidence.[54] This also holds true for the role of the Chairman; moreover investigation of this question is hindered by the figure of Mao Tse-tung and his unqiue role in Chinese Communist history. Perhaps the issue can only be dealt with satisfactorily when the passage of time allows a comparative analysis of Mao, Hua, and succeeding occupants of the senior position in the Politburo. A tendency to overrate Mao as a source of Chinese foreign policy initiatives and decisions until well into the 1970s has begun to subside in research. Michel Oksenberg's more general analysis of Mao's role in policy making indicates an interventionist stance, constrained or occasionally facilitated by the role expectations of the public, the bureaucracy, and his immediate associates in the senior ranks of the Party.[55] In relation to foreign policy, however, lack of any deep interest in all but the broadest brushstrokes of the world political picture tend to suggest a more sporadic engagement by Mao. Where he did turn his attention to foreign affairs, observers have remarked on a high degree of risk taking in Chinese policy.[56] In the case of the Taiwan Straits crisis of 1958, for example, recently available materials give evidence of considerable Party criticism of Mao on this point.[57]

Complexity and specialisation on the government side challenge the thesis of sustained Politburo direction, or of a decisive role by Mao even before his relinquishing of the chairmanship of the republic in 1959. The Ministry of Foreign Affairs is the most important, as well as the most studied, organ of the official foreign policy machinery. Its structure is similar to that of foreign ministries in other countries. Geographical departments are currently divided into (1) African, (2) American and Oceanic, (3) Asia, (4) Soviet Union and East European, (5) West Asian and North African, and (6) West European Affairs. Functional departments comprise (1) Consular Affairs, (2) the General Office, (3) Information, (4) International Organisations and Conferences and Treaty and Law, (5) Personnel, (6) Political Affairs and (7) Protocol.[58] This organisational layout is perhaps significant because of its ordinariness: there is no institutional embodiment here of Party thinking on the structure of the international system.

Diplomatic missions abroad are now more numerous than at any other period of China's history. At the beginning of the Cultural Revolution, China had ties with 46 countries. During its course, all but one of China's 41 ambassadors were recalled. As a result of foreign policy changes, which oversaw their return and the establishment of new diplomatic links, the Chinese by 1976 had official relations with 109 governments, had occupied since 1971 China's seat in the United Nations, had sent an ambassador to the European Communities in Brussels, and had exchanged Liaison Offices with the United States.[59] The State Council, the supreme government body, maintains a coordinating responsibility in relation to foreign policy and to foreign economic policy. As important in everyday terms are possibly the foreign affairs staffs directly under the Prime Minister. However, the superimposing of rational hierarchical notions on the governmental machinery is an impossible task. A full organisational description of its workings must also include the Ministry of National Defence, which clearly has a pivotal role considering the current agenda of Chinese foreign policy issues and the immediacy of the Soviet threat. The Ministries of Foreign Trade and of Economic Relations with Foreign Countries have their own geographical and functional subdivisions. There is a network of foreign bodies which include the Chinese import-export corporations for specific sectors or products and the China Committee for the Promotion of International Trade. With the expansion of trade links with Western countries in the 1970s, the foreign policy roles of other ministries, such as heavy industry or agriculture, have become more visible. Indeed sometimes lengthy delays in the negotiation of contracts with Western governments or corporations suggest a complex internal consultative process behind many decisions in this large area of China's foreign relations. Other bodies include the New China (Hsinhua) News Agency, which maintains offices in more than 50 countries, and which has in the past been credited by some observers with a quasi-diplomatic function; the Bank of China; and the Commission for Overseas Chinese Affairs.[60]

Do we have here, in the bifurcation of Chinese élites and of the values of 'red' versus 'expert'[61] a key to understanding variations in Chinese foreign policy? A straightforward cadre-diplomat conflict model is too simple, not least because allowance has to be made for groups and factions on either side. There are, firstly, clear signs of political leadership from the Party, how much depending in part on the issue. Individuals at Ministerial or Vice-Ministerial level can usually be expected to have had backgounds in Party work and to hold Central Committee or Politburo membership.[62] It would appear that the prestige and policy effectiveness of the Foreign Ministry has at times had more to do with the experience, values and preferences of the Minister himself than the capability of the professionals to push for an autonomous line. The obvious instance is Chou En-lai, though, as with Mao, evaluation of his role has to be qualified by consideration of his Party rank and personal standing. As Prime Minister, he maintained a low foreign policy profile during the early stages of the Cultural Revolution;[63] but in its aftermath took the leading part in the vigorous expansion of Chinese diplomatic links that preceded his death in 1976. Moreover, the Foreign Ministry has not been immune to the buffetings of domestic campaigns. During the Cultural Revolution, the Foreign Minister was subjected to intense criticism, to a pitch of personal humiliation and abuse, from radical factions which seized on the foreign affairs bureaucracy as a key target for attacks on revisionism.[64] Finally, reorganisation of the structure of the Foreign Ministry, for example in 1950, 1956, and 1962, seem to have coincided with, or even been precipitated by, broader policy changes originating in the Party.[65]

On the other hand, dependence on expertise has at times been paramount. The professional diplomatic corps can be considered a foreign policy actor in its own right by virtue of its access to information and the training and experience of its members. Personnel to staff some foreign affairs organisations are trained in the Foreign Languages Institutes, especially that in Peking. These began functioning again after the Cultural Revolution upsets in 1971. Greater emphasis was then given to the teaching of Western languages.[66] The image of a China either blinkered by ideology or else blissfully ignorant of the world outside cannot be substantiated, and probably could not even before the changes of the 1970s. The Foreign Ministry now has extensive political reports from embassies at its disposal, and in addition culls information from a broad range of foreign journalistic, academic and official sources. Detailed news analyses circulate among more restricted official audiences in China. Face to face encounters of Chinese with Asian or Western officials invariably indicate a well informed grounding. Chou En-lai himself displayed a remarkable record of continuity of detailed grasp of foreign affairs from before 1949 to 1976. And knowledge of the career background, linguistic competences, and negotiating skills of senior and middle ranking officials is not consonant with the view of Chinese diplomats as the docile instruments of the Party's will.[67]

The political significance of the People's Liberation Army, the third institutional pillar, in Chinese internal development and foreign policy has received considerable attention, though disagreement persists on the part of analysts as to how much influence should properly to attributed to it. Traditionally, from the beginnings of the Communist movement in China, the armed forces have tended to take a back seat to the Party in the drive either to modernisation or to the inculcation of revolutionary zeal in the masses. 'Politics in command' has been the operational motif more consistently than has Mao's alternative, if not entirely unambiguous, proposition that political power grows out of the barrel of a gun. There was pervasive PLA influence on politics during the civil war period, when indeed the role of the army became at times a matter of contention within the Party. As military leader, however, and later Commander of the PLA, Chu Teh from 1928 took the lead in emphasising the foremost role of the Party's leadership, and in particular of Mao as its head.

But even before the establishment of the People's Republic in 1949, senior army personnel continued nevertheless to take part in political decisions by virtue of their positions as Party members; and the military generally undertook important functions in relation to non-military matters, including at times civilian administration, assisting in the process of recovery of economic production, and in mobilisation and propaganda work at the mass level. Both these aspects — the intertwining of military with party and state offices, and the broader economic, political and educational role of the armed forces — have continued as features of the Communist political system.[68] It could be argued — depending on one's view of the capacity of Mao to control and direct events — that this pattern was not substantially upset by the initial upheavals of the Cultural Revolution. The two factors in the equation are, on the one hand, the Maoist goal of eradicating during the course of a long uphill struggle all remaining revisionist elements in the Party, and the use of the PLA as the chosen, and relatively incorrupt, instrument for this task; and, on the other hand, the ambitions of certain army factions, notably that identified with the figure of Lin Piao, later formally designated as Mao's heir apparent. The subsequent spread of military authority in Peking and in the provinces, in industry and agriculture, education and science, and party and government, has been well documented. In particular, the virtual destruction of the upper provincial levels of administration during the Cultural Revolution led to renewed army strength throughout many areas of China. Serious inroads into this power began to be evident at least from 1973, with evidence of stronger assertions of authority by the centre from 1974;[69] but the part played by the military in the rise of Hua two years later indicates a continuing and powerful voice in Chinese policy making.

The authority of the armed forces has also been shaped by the external setting facing Chinese leaders after 1949. More particularly, the Cultural Revolution coincided with the increasingly apparent dual threat to China's security posed both by the war in Vietnam and, more importantly, by continued Sino-Soviet dissension. Chinese commentary and official statements during the late 1960s became increasingly coloured by the simplistic propositions put forward by Lin in his *Long Live the Victory of the People's War* (1965), the main argument of which has been noted in an earlier section of this chapter. The upshot was greater emphasis in analyses appearing in China on the role of the PLA in planning and managing crucial areas of China's foreign relations. The military's influence can be seen in a number of specific policy sectors. Particularly after the second Chinese atomic test in 1965, statements increasingly drew attention to the primary role of the army in working on the development of China's nuclear programme. In relation to specific countries, the influence of the military's voice has varied, assuming prominence in issues touching on defence of Chinese territory, weapons procurement from Western countries, or the countering of Soviet influence.

Finally, at a fourth level, the regional dimension of Chinese politics has foreign policy significance. Partly because of readier accessibility of data at local rather than at central levels, research into Chinese urban and provincial politics has been in recent years a flourishing subfield. An unpublished study of 1975 has shown that Kwangtung province has a broad range of identifiable interests that intrude upon China's external environment.[70] The provinces have roles in relation to border defence and foreign trade, and foreign affairs offices are maintained at both provincial and municipal levels.[71]

We have suggested that a wide assortment of party, state, military and provincial actors potentially have some influence over the making of Chinese foreign policy. This may be relatively uncontroversial. The more contentious issue has to do with the relationships which exist between these actors. Most studies of Chinese foreign policy, at least until the late 1960s or early 1970s, tended to rely on some version of the totalitarian model to structure inter-actor relations. Centralised direction from a small leadership group in the party, the Standing Committee of the Politburo, was assumed; government organs, including the Foreign Ministry, were viewed as playing ancillary or merely implementing roles; the ideas of the men in the senior leadership of the party took on primary explanatory significance; domestic political constraints were felt to exert negligible influence over the leadership's freedom of manoeuvre; foreign policy decision making was seen as a process intimately connected with the Party; and the relative immutability of the policy process was held to be affected, on balance, neither by internal differences of outlook on the part of various actors nor by diversity in the stock of foreign policy issues facing the Chinese.[72] Intuitions as to the deficiencies of this approach, which bore resemblances to the centralist pattern of foreign policy making projected in the Chinese media, have rested on its exaggeration of the coercive power and administrative capacity of a handful of individuals, its inability to account satisfactorily for the complex range of political relationships apparent in Chinese society, its underlying assumption that the way large organisations acted in China was completely different from anything we knew about their workings in other contexts, and its failure to allow for the possibility of change.

At least two kinds of solutions to this dilemma have been found. Some factionalist models can be considered refinements of the totalitarian view. Even a Stalinist model can make allowance for, even highlight, personality clashes between rival contenders for leadership positions and power plays by ambitious individuals and factions. Similarly, Chinese accounts, while taking care to combat factionalism, also emphasise the dialectical quality of the decision process at all levels of the Party and the requirement, by implication, for conflicting opinions. Opinion, Schurmann has observed, 'is a commonly used word in the Chinese Communist vocabulary. Everyone must have "opinions", for it is only thus that "discussion" and "struggle" can take place. Moreover, at the inception of discussion, opinions must be divergent, then gradually fall into two opposite directions, and finally be resolved'.[73] Evidence of factionalism, or proto-factionalism, *can* be interpreted, then, as fully consistent with, and marginal to, an essentially authoritarian decision making system. And intra-party conflicts in China have often had foreign policy, and particularly Sino-Soviet, aspects, for example in the case of the power struggles culminating in the purging of Kao Kang in 1954, Marshal Peng Te-huai in 1959, or Lin Piao in 1971. Uri Ra'anan's analysis of internal party differences on Vietnamese and Sino-Soviet issues in the mid-1960s, moreover, indicates the existence of an interesting cross-cutting factional conflict. The view of a simple moderate-extremist clash needed qualification to account for the caution and restraint towards the West being advocated by Mao and Lin as compared with the more adventurous line being

131

urged by Liu Shao-ch'i, Teng Hsiao-p'ing, and Lo Jui-ching.[74] Similarly, the complex shifts of fortune between party factions betwen 1969 and 1977 — a period which comprised the end of the Cultural Revolution, its continuation in the form of the anti-rightist campaign against Confucius, the anti-leftist campaign against the 'gang of four' following Mao's death, the consolidation of Hua's position, and the rehabilitation of Teng — were played out against a background of Sino-Soviet tension, intensification and then termination of hostilities in Vietnam, and rapprochement with the United States. All presented issues which became the substance of internal party disputes.

The Cultural Revolution, indeed, gave totalitarian models a blow from which they have not recovered and ushered in a variety of conflict models of Chinese policy processes.[75] The implications for the study of Chinese foreign policy are still being worked out. Enough is known of group interests, for example, to permit the design of simulation models of Chinese policy making. At their simplest, these could incorporate the security and defence concerns of the PLA, and the goals of various factions within it;[76] the interests of different branches of the Foreign Ministry and of the foreign trade bureaucratic network; and the more ideologically-structured aims of party bureaucracies. It seems clear, moreover, that quite different kinds of processes may operate in different areas, such as Overseas Chinese policy, border state policy, international technical cooperation policy, or foreign aid policy.

Too great a scholarly interest in 'high' policy issues and in top party echelons and intrigues has obscured much of importance in China's orientation to foreign affairs. A characteristic response of Western 'old China hands' in 1948-9 was that the Communist Party would be unable, despite support from the Chinese peasantry and middle classes, to overcome when in power the political and economic organisation of more than two millennia based on local levels. This perspective, whether from a bias of sympathy with or antipathy towards the reforming and modernising goals of the Communists, tended to be edged out of research during the 1950s as factors like thought reform, purges, the role of the PLA in internal politics, and the link with the Soviet Union, directed attention more towards the centre and to the apparent capacity of modern technology to transcend, with some exceptions, the obstructive force of Chinese tradition. It seems implausible, however, that in China the local and provincial level can so snugly be fitted into an overall centralist framework, whether in relation to politics, economics or foreign policy. As one analyst noted in 1974, it quickly becomes evident that 'China's' foreign relations concerns are more rooted in provincial and sub-provincial 'enterprise' interests than in central government interests. ... Perhaps as much as half of the total physiology of Chinese foreign affairs involves the foreign trade enterprise offices. ... They, not the Ministry of Foreign Trade, account for most trade contact work and hence more Chinese foreign affairs. Whose interests do they reflect? China's? Or perhaps they represent a less central, more variegated pattern of group demands.[77]

Viewed from the bottom up, as it were, the shape of Chinese politics and of Chinese approaches to foreign relations takes on much more the spirit of 'perpetual political effervescence' that General de Gaulle described as France's hallmark, and much less the dull monotony of directives produced at a distant centre out of the interplay of leaders' squabbling.

Environment and foreign policy

Consideration of the external influences on the foreign policy of a given country forms an integral part of the study of international relations, and increasingly of comparative politics and public policy.[78] But in practice this had not been true of the study of Chinese foreign policy. Two possible reasons are worth noting. Firstly, there are difficulties of definition. Does foreign policy arising from Chinese factional dispute concerning Soviet motivations originate in an 'internal' or an 'external' factor? Secondly, there has been a suspicion that for all practical purposes the Chinese political system can be considered as having resilient boundaries that effectively shelter decision makers from influences that might arise within Chinese society or across the Chinese border. That the protective shields of states might be less effective than this is one inference from the growing body of research on transnational relations and the nature of environmental influences on state behaviour.

The Sino-Soviet split, for example, involved more than the gradual growing apart of two states formerly allies. In the terms used by James Rosenau in his discussion of linkage politics, China in the 1950s could be considered a penetrated political system. Participants on its political processes included members of another polity who, formally or otherwise, then shared authority to allocate its values.[79] What Rosenau has identified as an emulative process was also clearly evident in Chinese attempts to adapt lessons from the Soviet experience, with adjustments for Chinese conditions, in a variety of policy areas, including foreign policy stands on major world issues.[80] This, however, is a long way from asserting that China during the decade until 1960, when the Soviet Union withdrew assistance from the Chinese, was in some sense 'dominated' by the Soviets, or that Chinese foreign policy followed directives from Moscow. While public statements from China tended to echo Soviet pronouncements, the course of Chinese foreign policy towards the Soviet Union was a matter of continued debate in China from early in the 1950s; and the length of time needed in 1949-50 by Mao in Moscow to negotiate a satisfactory agreement can be taken perhaps as an indication of Chinese reservations about it that were only superficially smothered by the joint rhetoric of the cold war period.

The precise nature of the Soviet input into Chinese foreign policy making during the 1950s, then, still needs clarification and further research. One long term consequence may still be present in the fervour of the Chinese commitment to the principle of self reliance. It has recurred in policy areas as diverse as nuclear weapons development, support for foreign revolution, and the publishing of school textbooks,[81] and was reaffirmed with qualifications rather than demolished when China from 1977-78 began to focus attention on the role foreign, and particularly Western, capital would have to play in modernisation and industrialisation plans. Dependence theory, which emerged in response to problems of development in Latin America, may thus have a contribution to make to the study of Chinese foreign policy.[82] Certainly the background of Soviet relations with the Chinese Communists before 1949, the terms imposed on assistance from 1950, and the context of Soviet relations with the East European party-states in the 1950s, could have afforded the Chinese little hope of being able to forge an autonomous identity or to make an effective contribution to world communist decision making in the future.

Chinese foreign policy, moreover, has been made in a situation of perceived external threat varying from moderate to extreme over a period of some thirty years. Neglect of this factor, particularly in the United States, was formerly a weakness in the field. Writings sometimes left the impression that external events in the early and middle 1950s, such as continued Chinese Nationalist bombing raids on the mainland, United States intervention to prevent the liberation of Taiwan, retention by important Western states of official relations with the Kuomintang, the advance of United States land forces in Korea towards the Chinese border in 1950, public discussion by high United States officials of the option of invasion of China, or the designing of Western-Asian alliance systems aimed against China, had either no or minimal effects on Chinese foreign policy making other than a deterrent effect ruling out the practicality of presumed aggressive goals on the part of the leadership of the Chinese Communist Party. (Equally, revisionist cold war assessments, by attacking prevailing assumptions that United States policies were merely responsive, have tended to neglect the impact of Chinese statements and actions on Western perceptions and behaviour.[83]) The interaction processes giving rise to the spirals of mutually perceived threat between China and the United States, and later between China and the Soviet Union, still need more systematic investigation. The 'Soviet factor' has shaped Chinese policies in Asia, particularly in respect of India, Pakistan and Bangladesh, and Japan, and through Peking's opposition to Soviet plans for 'collective security' arrangements;[84] it has also affected Chinese policies in Latin America and Africa, and towards both Eastern[85] and Western[86] Europe.

External factors also have significance for internal Chinese debate and factionalism. The Western powers, in a sense, were good allies of Mao in his attempts in mid-1949 to persuade his more cautious colleagues of the virtues of pro-Soviet alignment. In 1946, Chou En-lai had told United States officials, 'Of course we will lean to one side, but how far depends upon you'.[87] While hypotheses relating the course of civil strife or factional conflict in a country to external variables are relatively common in the theoretical literature, such propositions have been rarer, and also more controversial, in the case of China studies. Both cohesive and fissiparous tendencies in China can be seen to have some outside roots. Repeated stress by the Party on unity and struggle — 'Practise Marxism, and not revisionism; unite and don't split; be open and aboveboard, and don't intrigue and conspire'[88] — are fully comprehensible only when due acount is taken of China's external environment. Schurmann has argued, with reference to the Sino-Soviet confrontation, that 'were it not for the developing war crisis, the Cultural Revolution would never have attained the furore that it did.'[89] While other factors were clearly operative in such a complex series of events, the international context was an important element precipitating, sustaining and terminating the Cultural Revolution, as well as prompting continued factional conflict in the 1970s.

Finally, Chinese foreign policy is made in the context of Chinese participation in a complex variety of interstate, intergovernmental and transnational systems. While we know a good deal from case studies of China's bilateral relationships with other states, we have considerably less understanding of the ways in which such networks of relationships affect China's external behaviour. The changing patterns of treaty making, for example, indicate a broad range of Chinese foreign policy interests,[90] and together with other factors suggest a kind of manoeuvering that stands comparison with classical balance of power politics in nineteenth century Europe. Particularly in view of the Sino-Soviet conflict, Chinese decision makers are impelled to move in the Asian international subsystem in ways that recall Mackinder's account of geopolitics in the Asian 'heartland'. While this is stretched, it would be interesting to discover just how much Chinese behaviour can be explained simply by reference to the structures and processes of the international system and its component subsystems. In the United Nations and its subsidiary organs from 1971, the Chinese took a generally cautious, and at first hesitant, approach, except in cases, such as Bangladesh's application for membership, that directly impinged on core Chinese interests. Declaratory support for the Group of 77 has been strong. But defence of the 200-mile economic zone concept in the negotiations on the Law of the Sea is as explicable in terms of strategic and economic self interest (the 'internal' factor) as of any obligations of mutual backing between China and Third World countries that might be held to constrain Peking's United Nations policy (the 'external' factor).[91] Neglect of China's transnational and transgovernmental relations leaves a large area in need of both research and conceptual clarification. The totality of China's cultural, scientific and technical relations with Western and developing countries, with Overseas Chinese communities, with Western travel or news organisations, or with foreign Friendship Associations and related groups, seems unlikely to be susceptible to sustained and centralised political direction from senior Party bodies in Peking.[92]

Conclusions

This short review has been able to note some striking successes by researchers in budging some of the road blocks that have habitually obstructed the study of Chinese foreign policy. Yet it has sometimes appeared as if the barriers to comparative analysis, and to empirical research informed by theory, have been rather more impenetrable. The reasons are not difficult to find.

136

One has been noted by Lucian Pye. It has, he has argued, 'become again obvious that the social sciences as developed for studying other societies lack the techniques for helping to explain Chinese developments'. This is in large part due to the secrecy which the Chinese impose over the dynamics of their political process.[93] Certainly a great deal of information is available about China. The Chinese put considerable emphasis on the dissemination of foreign language publications, while Western academic, official and journalistic bodies ensure a large and steady output of commentary and materials in translation. One estimate in 1970 was that between 150-200 pages of information about China were available daily to American Sinologists, translated into English, and including transcripts of the most important publicly accessible information.[94] Whether all of it is useful is another question. Some facts obviously are not available. Approaches to the study of China, indeed, have displayed considerable ingenuity in exploiting a variety of sources, including official publications, journals, refugee interviews, radio broadcast monitoring, economic indicators, exchanges with Chinese scholars, discussions with Soviet or Asian officials, and occasional scoops.[95] One inherent danger might therefore be that research can dissolve into mere intelligence gathering, a point on which Tong-eng Wang has criticised Chinese economic studies.[96] An eye to theory, then, is a useful correcting mechanism. Pessimism about the capability of available source materials to yield data against which to test middle-level propositions from the foreign policy literature seems premature.

Secondly, Chalmers Johnson has pictured the threat to the China scholar of becoming 'a supplier of raw materials, rather like a Bantu miner, chipping away at the cliff face of a South African mine, who is supposed to ship the unrefined ore off to the master goldsmiths living elsewhere — in this case, to "generalists", or "theorists", or "comparativists" toiling away in New Haven, Cambridge, Ann Arbor, or the Stanford "think tank", where the data will be processed'.[97] We are a long way from a constructive two-way flow of ideas and mutual criticism between Chinese foreign policy studies and either theoretical work or empirical research into related areas. The study of China can benefit from theoretical inputs and comparative perspectives; so, in turn, can broader endeavours gain by absorbing insights into the workings of the foreign policies of the communist states. Implicit universalising on the basis of evidence from Western systems alone, which has seemed to happen in some of the literature on bureaucratic politics, is not a sure foundation for the comparative study of foreign policy.[98]

Thirdly, the outlooks of scholars have been affected by the social context in which research has evolved. From the early historical encounters between China and the West sprang a sensitivity to the distinctiveness of Chinese life and thought — its uniqueness — that had to be consciously dampened with the emergence of a modern field of China studies in the United States.[99] Further, the historian's objection to the method of comparison, given a certain legitimacy within the China field by the predominant role of that discipline in its evolution, seemed then to be vindicated by the manner in which the Chinese state developed after 1949, and especially by its vociferous deviation later from the Soviet path. The education of researchers may also have been a factor; the effort of acquiring even modest linguistic capability does not endear the Sinologist to comparativist pleading.[100] The growth of China studies in the United States was also given impetus by policy considerations. High perceived threat, combined with the absence of diplomatic relations or other contacts, placed a premium on knowledge about China and strengthened the hunch that it constituted a special case. The scholarly interpretation of events immediately current took on new urgency. A high degree of consonance emerged between academic, official and public analyses of the character of the Chinese threat to United States interests. Attention to theory and the methods of social science was then inhibited by the disrepute into which such approaches had fallen by association with United States policies in South-East Asia and Latin America.

We would suggest, in conclusion, that the cultivation of greater interest in those forms of comparative investigation least threatening to the autonomy of Chinese area studies, and in theoretical innovations in foreign policy research, would be of considerable value for future progress. A simple distinction like that between individual and role behaviour, for example, as in Rosenau's 'pre-theory' foreign policy framework,[101] could cut inroads into the knowledge we have already of the biographies and career patterns of members of Party or government bodies, or of the views, policy preferences, biases and backgrounds of a Mao or a Teng, and help to play down the stress on personalities which has frequently marred research on China. Similarly, there is a need for resolution of the conflicting approaches to the modelling of the Chinese system — totalitarian, intergroup conflict, and so on — that have proliferated in the comparative politics literature of the last few years, and for greater knowledge of the interplay between the domestic and the external factors in the Chinese foreign policy process. China, it has often been suggested, is like no other country, not even any other communist country. Of the communist states, its size, history, and aspiration to global roles, make it most 'similar' to its chief enemy, the Soviet Union. But equally, like Yugoslavia, it has successfully fought off Soviet influence attempts and sought out ties in the nonaligned world; like Romania, it has established links with Western European nations as counterweights to the Soviets; like the GDR, it has battled with the problems of modernising and industrialising while retaining contact with ideological bases. Further afield, it has, like Egypt, coped with the problems of dealing with Russians on the spot and their intrigues; or, like France, of dealing with an alliance leader bent on drawing apparently wrong-headed conclusions about the significance of nuclear weapons technology. In a word, it is an ordinary country[102] wrestling, often inadequately, with the huge problems that confront it, and continually searching for the political forms and formulae that seem to hold out hope to doing a better job.

Notes

[1] *Peking Review*, No. 15, 12 April 1974, p.v. For recent treatments of the course of Chinese foreign policy, see Wang Gungwu, *China and the World since 1949: Impact of Independence, Modernity and Revolution* (London: Macmillan, 1977); John Gittings, *The World and China, 1922-1972* (London: Methuen, 1973); and Ian Wilson, ed., *China and the World Community* (Sydney: Angus and Robertson, 1973).

[2] *Peking Review*, No. 28, 24 June 1977, pp. 13-15. A Chinese official told the first group of foreign journalists to visit Sinkiang province that 'Nearly every day we have border problems with the Soviet Union at some point or another in our territory', (*The Times*, 4 July 1977).

[3] Cf. 'What is a superpower? A superpower is an imperialist country which everywhere subjects other countries to its aggression, interference, control, subversion or plunder and strives for world hegemony': Teng in *Peking Review*, No. 15, 12 April 1974, p.v.

[4] The background of Western attitudes and responses is discussed in A. Reichwein, *China and Europe: Intellectual and Artistic Contacts in the Eighteenth Century* (New York: Barnes and Noble, 1968, reprint of 1925 publications); Raymond Dawson, *The Chinese Chameleon: An Analysis of European Conceptions of Chinese Civilisation* (Oxford University Press, 1967); R. Iyer, ed., *The Glass Curtain between Asia and Europe* (Oxford University Press, 1965); H.R. Isaacs, *Scratches on Our Minds: American Images of China and India* (New York: Day, 1958); Akira Iriye, *Across the Pacific* (Harcourt, Brace and World, 1967); and A.T. Steele, *The American People and China* (New

York: McGraw-Hill, 1966). The part which images of China have played in the evolution of Western political thought is an intriguing footnote. For instance, J.S. Mill's understanding of China seems to have had an important influence on his critique of public opinion, see his *On Liberty* (New York: W.W. Norton, 1975), p. 68.

[5] See *Peking Review*, 40, 4 October 1974, pp. 16-18, on the new line linking Hunan and Kweichow.

[6] See for example Nicholas R. Lardy, 'Centralisation and Decentralisation in China's Fiscal Management', *China Quarterly*, 61, (March 1975), pp. 25-60 and his 'Economic Planning and Income Distribution in China', *Current Scene*, XIV, 11 (November 1976), pp. 1-12.

[7] A map of 1959 published by the Chinese, and later withdrawn, showed large areas of imperial China, including tributary areas, as lost territory. In some border negotiations, as with Burma and Pakistan, important concessions have been made with China. For the strategic significance of the nineteenth-century changes, see George Moseley, 'The Frontier Regions in China's Recent International Politics', in Jack Gray, ed., *Modern China's Search for a Political Form* (Oxford University Press, 1969), pp. 330-72.

[8] Robert Boardman, *Britain and the People's Republic of China, 1949-1974* (London: Macmillan, 1976), Ch. 2 and 4, pp. 9-27 and 56-76.

[9] See the classic exposition by C.P. Fitzgerald: 'The Chinese view of the world has not fundamentally changed: it has been adjusted to take account of the modern world, but only so far as to permit China to occupy, still, the central place in the picture' (*The Chinese View of Their Place in the World*, Oxford University Press, 1969, p. 71). See also Norton Ginsburg, 'On the Chinese Perception of a World Order', in Tang Tsou, ed., *China's Policies in Asia and America's Alternatives* (China in Crisis, Vol. 2) (University of Chicago Press, 1968), pp. 73-92, and U. Weiss, 'Imperial China's Tributary Trade and the Foreign Trade Policy of the PRC', *Asia Quarterly*, 1 (1976), pp. 35-68. For an entertaining and stimulating discussion of the issues see John Israel, 'Continuities and Discontinuities in the Ideology of the Great Proletarian Cultural Revolution', in Chalmers Johnson, ed., *Ideology and Politics in Contemporary China* (Seattle: University of Washington Press, 1973), pp. 3-46.

[10] The example, not the analogy, is from the discussion in Mark Elvin, *The Pattern of the Chinese Past* (Stanford University Press, 1973), p. 94.

[11] See for example Wang Gungwu, 'Juxtaposing Past and Present in China Today', *China Quarterly*, 61 (March 1975), pp. 1-24.

[12] The first Chinese responses to British recognition in 1950 drew attention to the nineteenth century and civil war records of the British Government. For instance, see 'China Will Judge British Policy by Deeds, Not Words', New China News Agency, January 17, 1950; 'Britain's Two-Faced Policy', *World Culture*, May 19, 1950; and John H. Weakland, 'Chinese Film Images of Invasion and Resistance', *China Quarterly*, 47 (July-September 1971).

[13] The argument from economic history to the nature of political power in China is developed in Karl Wittfogel, *Oriental Despotism: A Comparative Study of Total Power* (New Haven, Conn.: Yale University Press, 1957).

[14] J.D. Simmonds, *China's World: The Foreign Policy of a Developing State* (Canberra: ANU Press, 1970), pp. 134-5.

[15] Chinese statements in August 1974 and January 1975 put the figure at almost 800m. A 1975 figure of 938m. is given in US Congress, Joint Economic Committee, *China: A Reassessment of the Economy* (Washington: Government Printing Office, 1975); of 838.8m. including Taiwan in UN statistics; and of 934.6m. in Department of State, *The Planetary Product in 1975.* Special Report No. 33 (May 1977), p. 12. See further Alexander Eckstein, *China's Economic Revolution* (Cambridge University Press, 1977) and Audrey Donnithorne, *China's Economic System* (New York: Praeger, 1967).

[16] The major study on this point, emphasising Chinese definitions of national interest above ideological demands, is Peter Van Ness, *Revolution and Chinese Foreign Policy* (Berkeley: University of California Press, 1970).

[17] *Selected Works of Mao Tse-tung,* Vol. IV (Peking: Foreign Languages Press, 1961), p. 415.

[18] 'The Foolish Old Man Who Removed the Mountains', speech of June 11, 1945 (Peking: Foreign Languages Press, 1972), cited by Alan Lawrance, *China's Foreign Relations since 1949* (London: Routledge and Kegan Paul, 1975), p. 21.

[19] *People's Daily,* January 21, 1964; *Peking Review,* 4, 24 January 1964, p. 7.

[20] 'Long Live the Victory of People's War', *People's Daily,* September 2, 1965; *Peking Review,* 3 September 1965, pp. 9-30.

[21] As in Mao's 'If you want to know the taste of a pear, you must change the pear by eating it yourself' (*On Practice, 1937*).

[22] John Bryan Starr, *Ideology and Culture: An Introduction to the Dialectic of Contemporary Chinese Politics* (New York: Harper and Row, 1973). See also Richard M. Pfeffer, 'Mao and Marx in the Marxist-Leninist Tradition: A Critique of "the China field" and a Contribution to a Preliminary Reappraisal', *Modern China,* 2, 4 (October 1976), pp. 421-60; and the response by Stuart R. Schram, *Modern China,* 3, 2 (April 1977). Frederic Wakeman has criticised the view of Maoist ideology as being simply 'leftist' or 'idealist' by comparison with European marxisms for its retarding effects on our understanding of Chinese foreign policy; see his 'The Use and Abuse of Ideology in the Study of Contemporary China', *China Quarterly,* 61 (March 1975), p. 141.

[23] Johnson, ed., op. cit., p. v.

[24] Robert A. Dahl, *Modern Political Analysis,* 2nd ed. (Englewood Cliffs, N.J.: Prentice-Hall, 1970), p. 42. See also Willard A. Mullins, 'On the Concept of Ideology in Political Science', *American Political Science Review,* LXVI, 2 (June 1972), pp. 498-510; Archie Brown and Jack Gray, eds., *Political Culture and Political Change in Communist States* (London: Macmillan, 1977); and

Kenneth Jowitt, 'An Organisational Approach to the Study of Political Culture in Marxist-Leninist Systems', *American Political Science Review*, LXVIII, 3 (September 1974), pp. 1171-91. On the foreign policy implications of Maoism, see Philip L. Bridgham, 'The International Impact of Maoist Ideology', in Johnson, ed., op. cit., pp. 326-51; A.M. Halpern, 'The Foreign Policy Uses of the Chinese Revolutionary Model', *China Quarterly*, 7 (1961), pp. 1-16; Chalmers Johnson, *Autopsy on People's War* (Berkeley: University of California Press, 1974); Vincent Chen, 'Mao's "United Front" as Applied in China's Diplomacy', in Hsiung, op. cit., pp. 105-36; and Richard Lowenthal, 'Soviet and Chinese Communist World Views', in Donald W. Treadgold, ed., *Soviet and Chinese Communism: Similarities and Differences* (Seattle: University of Washington Press, 1967), pp. 374-404.

[25] On Soviet views, see A. James Melnick, 'Soviet Perceptions of the Maoist Cult of Personality', *Studies in Comparative Communism*, IX, 1/2 (Spring-/Summer 1976), pp. 129-44; George Ginsburgs, 'Soviet Critique of the Maoist Political Model', in Hsiung, op.cit., pp. 137-62; E. Stuart Kirby, *Russian Studies of China* (London: Macmillan, 1976); and W.W. Kulski, *The Soviet Union in World Affairs: A Documented Analysis, 1964-1972* (Syracuse University Press, 1973), Ch. 10, pp. 346-405. I have developed the theme of the comparability of United States and Soviet perceptions of China in 'Expectations of Aggression in Interstate Conflict', Paper presented to the Annual Conference of the Political Studies Association, St. Catherine's College, Oxford, March 24-26, 1975.

[26] Richard H. Solomon, Mao's Revolution and the Chinese Political Culture (Berkeley: University of California Press, 1971), pp. 365-66.

[27] Ibid. See also Mao's discussion of the relation between economic construction and defence in 'On the Ten Major Relationships', cited in *Peking Review*, No. 1, 1 January 1977, pp. 10-25.

[28] Melvin Gurtov, 'The Taiwan Straits Crisis Revisited: Politics and Foreign Policy in Chinese Motives', *Modern China*, II, 1 (January 1976), pp. 49-50. See also Allen S. Whiting, 'New Light on Mao: 3. Quemoy 1958: Mao's Miscalculations', *China Quarterly*, No. 62 (June 1975), pp. 263-70.

[29] 'Lu Hsu-chang's Statement to British Businessmen on Cultural Revolution', *China Trade and Economic Newsletter*, No. 139 (May 1967), pp. 8-9; 'China's Foreign Affairs Establishment', *Current Scene*, XIV, 7 (July 1976), p. 9.

[30] See G.H. Quester, 'On the Identification of Real and Pretended Communist Military Doctrine', *Journal of Conflict Resolution*, X (1966), pp. 172-79. On the Chinese defensive military posture, see William W. Whitson, ed., *The Military and Political Power in China in the 1970s* (New York: Praeger, 1972).

[31] Gregory J. Clark, *In Fear of China* (Melbourne: Lansdowne, 1967), p. 106.

[32] Hsinhua News Agency, 29 December 1971. Cf. the earlier 'British Imperialism is at the End of its Rope', *People's Daily*, 16 January 1968.

[33] Cited by A. Huck, *The Security of China* (London: Chatto and Windus,

1970), p. 51.

[34] To name but a few situations. For a recent assessment see Alaba Ogunsanwo, *China's Policy in Africa, 1958-1971* (Cambridge University Press, 1975).

[35] This is one possible interpretation of Soviet behaviour, suggested to the author by Professor Michael K. MccGwire.

[36] See, for example, William E. Ratliff, 'Communist China and Latin America, 1949-1971', *Asian Survey*, XII, 10 (October 1972), pp. 846-63, and S. D'Ignazio and Daniel Tretiak, 'Latin America: How Much do the Chinese Care?', *Studies in Comparative Communism* (1972), pp. 36-46.

[37] C.P. Fitzgerald, *China and South-east Asia since 1945* (London: Longman, 1973), p. 90. See also Stephen Fitzgerald, *China and the Overseas Chinese: A Study of Peking's Changing Policy, 1949-1970* (Cambridge University Press, 1972).

[38] This simple generalisation obviously requires qualification. For some recent assessments see David Mozingo, *Chinese Policy towards Indonesia, 1949-1967* (Ithaca: Cornell University Press, 1976) and Wayne Best, 'Chinese Relations with Burma and Indonesia', *Asian Survey*, XV, 6 (June 1975), pp. 473-87. Chinese appreciation of the force of south-east Asian nationalism is stressed in Seymour Topping, *Journey between Two Chinas* (New York: Harper and Row, 1972), p. 176. See also the references at note 84, below.

[39] See, for example, Alan P.L. Liu, *Communication and National Integration in Communist China* (University of California Press, 1971), pp. 188 and 193 ff.

[40] Daniel Tretiak, 'Is China Preparing to "Turn out"? Changes in Chinese Levels of Attention to the International Environment', *Asian Survey*, XI, 3 (March 1971), pp. 219-37.

[41] For example, James C.F. Wang, *The People's Liberation Army in Communist China's Political Development: A Contingency Analysis of the Military's Perception and Verbal Symbolization during the Cultural Revolution, 1966-1969*, University of Hawaii, PhD dissertation, 1971.

[42] See for example Robert Simmons' finding of different clusterings of interests represented within the Foreign Ministry and the Party's Central Committee, based on an analysis of World Culture and People's Weekly ('The Concept of "Alliance" as a Tool in the Study of Chinese Foreign Policy', in R.L. Dial, ed., *Advancing and Contending Approaches to the Study of Chinese Foreign Policy* (Halifax: Centre for Foreign Policy Studies, Dalhousie University, 1974), pp. 253-90.

[43] For example, Milton A. Ochsner, *Chinese Communist Attitudes towards the Soviet Union, 1949-1965: A Content Analysis of Official Documents*, University of Oklahoma, PhD dissertation, 1968.

[44] See Linda D. Dillon, Bruce Burton, and Walter C. Soderlund, 'Who was the Principal Enemy? Shifts in Official Chinese Perceptions of the Superpowers, 1968-69', *Asian Survey*, XVII (5), May 1977, pp. 456-73. For a comparative

study of Soviet and Chinse perceptions of the United States in the context of alliance theory, see Ole R. Holsti, 'External Conflict and Internal Cohesion: The Sino-Soviet Case', in Jan F. Triska, ed., *Communist Party-States: Comparative and International Studies* (New York: Bobbs-Merrill, 1969), pp. 337-53.

[45] On content, see William E. Griffith, 'On Esoteric Communication' *Studies in Comparative Communism*, III 1 (January 1970), pp. 47-54, and David Liden, 'Grain Production in China, 1950-1970: A Case Study in Political Communication', *Asian Survey*, XV, 6 (June 1975), pp. 510-29. On internal networks, see Michel Oksenberg, 'Methods of Communication within the Chinese Bureaucracy', *China Quarterly*, No. 57 (January/March 1974), pp. 1-39, and Alan P.L. Liu, 'Control of Public Information and its Effects on China's Foreign Affairs', *Asian Survey*, xiv, 10 (October 1974), pp. 936-51.

[46] For example, Allen S. Whiting, *The Chinese Calculus of Deterrence: India and Indochina* (Ann Arbor: University of Michigan Press, 1975), p. xix.

[47] On Chinese approaches to policy making, see Michel C. Oksenberg, 'Policy Making under Mao, 1949-68: An Overview', in John M.H. Lindbeck, ed., *China: Management of a Revolutionary Society* (Seattle: University of Washington Press, 1971), pp. 79-115; P.H. Chang, *Power and Policy in China* (Pennsylvania State University Press, 1975); and James R. Townsend, *Politics in China* (Boston: Little, Brown, 1974).

[48] Franz Schurmann, *Ideology and Organisation in Communist China*, 2nd ed. (University of California Press, 1968), p. 173.

[49] Robert North, *The Foreign Relations of China* (Belmont: Dickenson, 1969), p. 68.

[50] Harold C. Hinton, *An Introduction to Chinese Politics* (New York: Praeger, 1973), pp. 257-58.

[51] For a fuller discussion see Schurmann, op. cit., Ch. II, pp. 105-72; Townsend, op. cit., Ch. III, VI, VII; Jürgen Domes, *The Internal Politics of China, 1949-72* (London: Hurst, 1973); John W. Lewis, ed., *Party Leadership and Revolutionary Power in China* (Cambridge University Press, 1970); and James P. Harrison, *The Long March to Power: A History of the Chinese Communist Party, 1921-1972* (New York: Praeger, 1972).

[52] Schurmann, op. cit., pp. 140-42.

[53] Simmonds, op. cit., pp.134-35.

[54] Donald W. Klein, 'The Management of Foreign Affairs in Communist China', in Lindbeck, op. cit., p. 331. Evidence from Chinese media reports of Chinese official meetings with foreign Communist Party leaders, he adds, leads consistently to the Party Secretariat as the heart of party control of foreign affairs, subject to overall guidance by the Politburo and its Standing Committee (pp. 331-32).

[55] Oksenberg, op. cit. For recent stocktakings, see Dick Wilson, ed., *Mao Tse-tung in the Scales of History* (Cambridge University Press, 1977); Lucian W. Pye, *Mao Tse-tung: The Man in the Leader* (New York: Basic Books, 1976);

144

and *Mao Tse-tung Unrehearsed: Talks and Letters, 1956-1971*, ed. Stuart Schram (Penguin, 1974).

[56] Confusion about whether the subject of observations is 'China' or 'Mao' muddies the picture. But see Harding's account: one can predict 'not that Mao will embark on reckless foreign policy initiatives but that he will select policy options that 1 facilitate the maintenance of strict central control over their execution, 2 are reversible and thus preserve flexibility, and 3 provide opportunities to assess the outcome before irrevocably committing China to their pursuit' (Harry Harding, Jr, 'Maoist Theories of Policy-Making and Organization', in Thomas W. Robinson, ed., *The Cultural Revolution in China* (Berkeley: University of California Press, 1971), p. 131, n. 47. Compare Whiting's analysis based on (1) early signalling, (2) 'worst case' assumptions, and (3) deliberate timing (Whiting, *The Chinese Calculus of Deterrence*, op. cit.)

[57] Whiting, 'New Light on Mao', op. cit.

[58] 'China's Foreign Affairs Establishment', *Current Scene*, xiv, 7 (July 1976), pp. 9-11.

[59] Ibid. On the foreign policy machinery, see further Klein, op. cit.: Simmonds, op. cit., pp. 63-74; Donald Klein, 'Peking's Evolving Ministry of Foreign Affairs', *China Quarterly*, October-December 1960; and his 'The Men and Institutions behind China's Foreign Policy', in Roderick MacFarquhar, ed., *Sino-American Relations, 1949-1971* (New York: Praeger, 1972); and Roger L. Dial, *Chinese Foreign Policy: Towards a Framework for Causal and Comparative Analysis*, University of California, Berkeley, PhD dissertation, 1972.

[60] There are also important party bureaucracies, for example the United Front Work Department of the Central Committee; the Overseas Chinese Department; and especially the International Liaison Department, which directs relations with other Communist Parties.

[61] Schurmann, op. cit., pp. 51-3; and John A, Kringen, 'An Exploration of the "Red-Expert" Issue in China through Content Analysis', *Asian Survey*, XV, 8 (August 1975), pp. 693-707.

[62] Simmonds, op. cit., Appendix V, p. 235; Klein (see fn. 59, above); Roger L. Dial, 'An Organization Decision-Making Approach to Chinese Foreign Policy: Towards an Explanation of Revisionism', in Dial, ed., op. cit., Appendix 2, pp. 313-15.

[63] Thomas W. Robinson, 'Chou En-lai and the Cultural Revolution in China', in Robinson, op. cit., pp. 165-312.

[64] Melvin Gurtov, 'The Foreign Ministry and Foreign Affairs in the Chinese Cultural Revolution', in Robinson, op. cit., pp. 316-66.

[65] Simmonds, op. cit., pp. 133-34.

[66] The teaching of international relations also began again at Peking University the previous autumn. The wide range of western and other foreign teaching material available in the library was confirmed to the author by Paul Evans, a doctoral candidate in the Department of Political Science, Dalhousie Univer-

sity, in April 1977, following a visit to the campus during the previous summer.

[67] Klein, 'The Management of Foreign Affairs', pp. 328-30; Henry G. Schwarz, 'The *Ts'an-k'ao Hsiao-shi*: How Well Informed are Chinese officials about the Outside World?', *China Quarterly*, 27 (July-September 1966), pp. 54-83; and Oksenberg, 'Methods of Communication.'

[68] Parts of this discussion have been adapted from Immanuel C.Y. Hsu, *The Rise of Modern China*, 2nd ed. (London: Oxford University Press, 1975), pp. 856 ff. For background studies, see John Gittings, *The Role of the Chinese Army* (London: Oxford University Press, 1967), and Ellis Joffe, *Party and Army: Professionalism and Political Control in the Officer Corps, 1949-64* (Cambridge: Harvard University Press, 1965). The institutional set-up is well described by Townsend (op. cit., pp. 95 ff.) See further Gregory J. Terry, 'The "Debate" on Military Affairs in China, 1957-1959', *Asian Survey*, xvi, 8 (August 1975), pp. 788-813.

[69] Paul H.B. Godwin, 'The PLA and Political Control in China's Provinces: A Structural Analysis', *Comparative Politics,* 9, 1 (October 1976), pp. 1-20.

[70] David L. Cook, *The Foreign Policy Interests and Actions of Kwangtung Province, 1949-65*, Dalhousie University: MA thesis, 1975.

[71] Audrey Donnithorne, 'The Internal Development and External Relations of China with Special Reference to the Future of Sino-Soviet Relations', *Australian Outlook* (August 1969); and her *China's Economic System* (New York: Praeger, 1967); Klein, 'The Management of Foreign Affairs', p. 313. On the general literature, see Lardy, *op. cit.*; and Frederick C. Teiwes, *Provincial Leadership in China: The Cultural Revolution and its Aftermath* (Ithaca, NY.: Cornell University Press, 1974).

[72] This argument is developed in Robert Boardman, 'Themes and Explanation in Sinology', in Dial, *Advancing and Contending Approaches*, pp. 5-50.

[73] Schurmann, op. cit., pp. 54-5, n. 30.

[74] Uri Ra'anan, 'Peking's Foreign Policy "Debate", 1965-1966', in Tsou, op. cit., pp. 23-72.

[75] Richard M. Pfeffer, 'Serving the People and Continuing the Revolution', *China Quarterly*, No. 52 (October-December 1972), pp. 620-53; Y.C. Chang, *Factional and Coalition Politics in China: Rebuilding of the Communist Party* (New York: Praeger, 1977); and Alan P.L. Liu, *Political Culture and Group Conflict in Communist China* (Santa Barbara: Clio Press, 1976).

[76] See William Pang-yu Ting, 'A Longitudinal Study of Chinese Military Factionalism, 1949-1973', *Asian Survey*, XV, 10 (October 1975), pp. 896-910; and William Whitson with Huang Chen-hsia, *The Chinese High Command: A History of Communist Military Politics* (New York: Praeger, 1973).

[77] Roger L. Dial, 'The Interest Group Approach in the Analysis of Chinese Foreign Policy', in Dial, *Advancing and Contending Approaches*, p. 371.

[78] See for example Richard L. Siegel and Leonard B. Weinberg, *Comparing Public Policies: United States, Soviet Union, and Europe* (Homewood, Ill.:

Dorsey, 1977), Ch. 3, pp. 52-100.

[79] James N. Rosenau, ed., *Linkage Politics: Essays on the Convergence of National and International Systems* (New York: Free Press, 1969), pp. 44-9.

[80] Ibid.

[81] On the last, see *Peking Review*, No. 1, 4 January 1974, p. 29.

[82] For a review, see for example Harry R. Targ, 'Global Dominance and Dependence: Post-industrialism, and International Relations Theory', *International Studies Quarterly*, XX, 3 (September 1976), pp. 461-82. The special factors in the Chinese case were that dependence was voluntarily entered into, and could be terminated.

[83] On rival models of the dynamics of Chinese politics in debates in the 1950s, see Robert Boardman, 'Conflict in Western Perceptions of Change: Two Profiles of China', *British Journal of Political Science*, I, 2 (April 1971).

[84] See for example Alexander O. Ghebhardt, 'The Soviet System of Collective Security in Asia', *Asian Survey*, XIII, 12 (December 1973); Sheldon W. Simon, 'China, the Soviet Union, and the Continental Balance', *Asian Survey*, XIII, 7 (July 1973), pp. 647-58; Gene T. Hsiao, 'Prospects for a New Sino-Japanese Relationship', *China Quarterly*, No. 60 (October-December 1974), pp. 720-49; Chae-Jin Lee, *Japan Faces China: Political and Economic Relations in the Postwar Era* (Baltimore: Johns Hopkins, 1976); and William J. Barnds, 'China's Relations with Pakistan: Durability amidst Discontinuity', *China Quarterly*, No. 63 (September 1975), pp. 463-89.

[85] For example in the Sino-Romanian relationship; China's alignment with Albania began to split in 1977. On the background, see Robin Remington, 'China's Emerging Role in Eastern Europe', in Charles Gati, ed., *The International Politics of Eastern Europe* (New York: Praeger, 1976), pp. 82-102.

[86] The Chinese media continue to report favourably on any moves indicating a strengthening of hardware or resolve on the part of the NATO powers. Opposition to appeasement of the Soviet Union forms a bond between the Chinese and West European Conservatives. See for example 'Chairman Hua meets Mrs. Thatcher', *Peking Review*, No. 16, 15 April 1977, pp. 4-6.

[87] Cited by Allen S. Whiting, 'Foreign Policy of Communist China', in Roy C. Macridis, ed., *Foreign Policy in World Politics*, 4th ed. (Englewood Cliffs, N.J.: Prentice-Hall, 1972), p. 312. The remark was passed to him by a foreign service officer on the staff of Ambassador George C. Marshall.

[88] New Year message of *Renmin Ribao, Hongqi*, and *Jiefangjun Bao* as cited in *Peking Review*, No. 1, 4 January 1974.

[89] Schurmann, op. cit., p. 573. For a review of later factionalist struggle see Parris H. Chang, 'The Passing of the Maoist Era', *Asian Survey*, xvi, 11 (November 1976), pp. 997-1011.

[90] See for example Gary L. Scott, 'Treaties of the People's Republic of China: A Quantitative Analysis', *Asian Survey*, XIII, 5 (May 1973), pp. 496-512. Chinese approaches to international law generally are evaluated in Jerome Alan

Cohen and Hungdah Chiu, *People's China and International Law: A Documentary Study* (Princeton N.J.: Princeton University Press, 1974).

[91] John F. Copper, 'Peking on the Law of the Sea Conference', *China Report*, XI 1 (January-February 1975), p. 307; 'China's Stand on the question of Exploitation of International Seabed', *Peking Review*, No. 28, 8 July 1977, pp. 22-3.

[92] For an early discussion of this area generally, see Robert O. Keohane and Joseph S. Nye, Jr. *Transnational Relations and World Politics* (Cambridge: Harvard University Press, 1971).

[93] Lucian W. Pye, 'Generational Politics in a Gerontocracy: The Chinese Succession Problem', *Current Scene*, XIV, 7 (July 1976), pp. 1-2.

[94] Thomas W. Robinson, *China Data Retrieval: A Method for Computer-Assisted Indexing of Translated Mainland Chinese Material*, The RAND Corporation, RM-6332-PR (December 1970), pp. 1-2.

[95] Michel Oksenberg, 'Sources and Methodological Problems in the Study of Contemporary China', in A. Doak Barnett, ed., *Chinese Communist Politics in Action* (Seattle: University of Washington Press, 1969), pp. 577-606. There is a review of bibliographical and other materials in John T. Ma, 'Sources of Information: A Brief Survey', in Yuan-li Wu, ed., *China: A Handbook* (New York: Praeger, 1973), pp. 759 ff. Interviews with Chinese lawyers, historians and anthropologists are reported in *China Quarterly*, Nos. 61 (March 1975), pp. 118-26, and 60 (December 1974), pp. 767 ff., 775 ff. Klein refers as sources to interviews with Asian officials ('The Management of Foreign Affairs', p. 328, n. 22); and Whiting to interviews with Russians (*The Chinese Calculus of Deterrence*). Acquisition of classified military material produced fresh insights into the PLA (J. Chester Cheng, ed., *The Politics of the Chinese Red Army*, Stanford: Hoover Institution, 1966); and of Cultural Revolution materials into later political developments (*China Quarterly*, articles in Nos. 57, 60, 61, 62). Data collections in several areas are now basic resources: see for example Donald Klein and Anne B. Clark, ed., *Biographic Dictionary of Chinese Communism*, 1921-65 (Cambridge: Harvard University Press, 1971); and Douglas M. Johnston and Hungdah Chiu, ed, *Agreements of the People's Republic of China, 1949-65: A Calendar* (Cambridge: Harvard University Press, 1968).

[96] Tong-eng Wang, 'Some Suggestions for Chinese Economic Studies', *Asian Survey*, XIII 10 (October 1973), p. 946.

[97] Chalmers Johnson, 'Political Science and East Asian Area Studies', *World Politics*, XXVI, 4 (1974), p. 561. See further L.W. Pye, ed., *Political Science and Area Studies: Rivals or Partners* (Bloomington: University of Indiana Press, 1975).

[98] See for example the complaints of Peter R. Baehr, 'Pitfalls in the Study of Sources of Foreign Policy', Paper presented to the European Consortium for Political Research Workshop, London School of Economics and Political Science, 7-13 April 1975.

[99] The point is discussed by George E. Taylor, 'Special Report: The Joint Committee on Contemporary China, 1959-69', *Asian Studies Professional Review*, I, 1 (Fall 1971), p. 47.

[100] Though possession of language skills is still far from the rule in the United States; see the survey by Elizabeth Massey and Joseph Massey, 'Language Competence of American Specialists in China', *Asian Studies*, IV, 1/2 (Fall/Spring 1974-5), pp. 119-23. Materials are available in translation, but differences between the Western and the Chinese political vocabularies can be expected ultimately to set a limit to their utility. For a general discussion of problems in this area, see Mostafa H. Nagi, 'Language Variables in Cross-Cultural Research', *International Social Science Journal*, XXIX, 1 (1977), pp. 167-77.

[101] James N. Rosenau, 'Pre-Theories and Theories of Foreign Policy', republished in his *The Scientific Study of Foreign Policy* (New York: Free Press, 1971), pp. 95-150. Cf. the use made of the distinction in Oksenberg's 'Policy Making under Mao', op. cit.

[102] See Richard Rosecrance, ed., *America as an Ordinary Country: United States Foreign Policy in the Future* (Cornell University Press,1977).

6   Conclusions and suggestions for further study

HANNES ADOMEIT AND ROBERT BOARDMAN

It is appropriate at this stage to review the state of the proceedings. We set out (in the introductory essay) some of the main research problems involved in the comparative approach to the study of foreign policy making in communist states, and suggested some of the more important methodological questions arising in such study. Each of the four country charters then attempted to provide some answers. Although an endeavour of this kind, focusing on a limited number of countries and comparable factors falls short of formal comparative research within a rigid framework of analysis, it does go several steps beyond isolated case studies. Which factors, then, have been given prominence by the contributors to the present collection of essays, and what conclusions emerge from them?

The 'Soviet dimension' for all communist states other than the USSR can be dealt with first simply because of its pre-eminent place in the existing literature. Marsh's criticism of the wisdom of applying 'bloc' models to relations between the GDR and the Soviet Union is symptomatic of a wider discontent in recent communist studies. It has been prompted, certainly, by changes in the real world. The constraints on Brezhnev are more numerous, weightier and more complex than those on Stalin. Changes in the international atmosphere make it easier to focus research on such differentiations as may exist in the Soviet sphere of influence.

In the case of the GDR, Marsh points out that shifts of policy cannot be attributed solely to changes in the Soviet outlook. On some questions affecting the East European nations, most notably on the German issue, the GDR could be seen taking the lead in formulating policy stands and securing their wider acceptance by other states. The tit for tat arrangements of 1968-69, whereby the Soviet Union, among other things, obtained GDR financial participation in the exploitation of Siberian natural gas and acceptance for increased Soviet capital exports to the GDR, and the GDR achieved a greater voice in intra-bloc policies and a firm (though temporary) repudiation of Bonn's *Ostpolitik*, in an interesting extension of a kind of process that has parallels in other areas of Soviet-

150

East European relations. In a similar way, Laux's chapter highlights the various ways in which the Romanian leadership has been able at successive points to exploit tensions between China and the Soviet Union as a means of expanding the degree of diversification in its foreign economic and political relations. In the case of China after the signing of the 1950 treaty with the USSR, evidence tends to discount the view that Peking's policies were shaped largely by its neighbour. Strains were apparent at the time which, in retrospect, looks like a fundamental clash of national interests. These examples suggest that tendencies of autonomy and processes of differentiation away from Soviet dominance will continue to play an important role in national foreign policy making in Eastern Europe — *despite* the fact that the Soviet Union has made vigorous attempts in the wake of the Warsaw Pact intervention in Czechoslovakia in 1968 to tighten bloc discipline in the ideological and political sphere, and to promote 'socialist integration' in the economic sphere.

One way to explore further the Soviet dimension in foreign policy making in the individual East European states might be to adopt broad cross-system comparisons. Other, quite different, countries also have foreign policies constrained by the necessity of having to live with a large neighbour. One can readily think of Malawi, Finland, New Zealand, Nepal, Canada or Ireland. We may have here an alternative framework of comparison which would enable us to isolate the differing factors making for compliance and deviance in the Soviet-East European context. More of this later.

A related conclusion is that no one model can adequately cope with the variety of policy processes found in communist states. Analysts of Soviet policies have for some years found persuasive evidence of internal group interaction or 'interest group' participation in policy areas as diverse as agriculture, defence, education, criminal policy, and science. It is still very much a controversial question, however, to what extent such interaction and participation exists in the realm of Soviet foreign policy. Marsh's chapter in the present volume indicates the extent to which the GDR leadership's approach to foreign economic issues prompted internal disputes of a significant order between pro-Soviet factions and technical or functional specialists. Similarly, Boardman's chapter on the PRC brings out the ways in which the central policy question of the appropriate relationship with and response to the Soviet Union provided a crucial focus for differentiating contending groups and factions in the policy making arena, with far reaching implications for institutional structures and political change. The interesting exception to this general tendency, as far as the limited number of cases examined in this book is concerned, is Romania. Laux notes the existence of minority ethnic groups and others which might conceivably play some part in influencing policy or in constructing the domestic environment within which policy is made. She concludes, however, that there is little evidence of group interaction or conflict in the foreign policy domain. Centralism and personalism better characterise political processes under Ceausescu. In a separate study, she observes that Ceausescu himself made all major speeches, 93 per cent of these being on foreign policy topics.

This contrast between Romania and China in particular is instructive. Both have aimed at achieving varying degrees of autonomy in policy making from the Soviet Union, both have tended to be more Leninist than the USSR in their approach to ideological and theoretical questions, and both have for long periods been identified with the personal leadership styles of one major figure. The differing nature of the perceived external threat may here have been an important factor making for variation. Ceausescu's attempt to draw policy implications from the imputed '2,000-year-old threat' to Romania territorial integrity mirrors neatly Chinese historical memories of foreign invasion. Whereas this device seems to have been relatively successful in the Romanian case in promoting or ensuring cohesion, attempts by Chinese leaderships appear to have met with varying success. The threatening external situation, as perceived in Peking, may rather have been partly responsible for internal upheaval, for example during the Cultural Revolution. The curve of response to perceived external threat may, then, bend in some unexpected ways.

The role of bureaucracies in the foreign policy processes of communist countries raises equally controversial issues as the question of group interaction and participation. Growing interest during the 1970s in 'bureaucratic politics' as a conceptual lens for the analysis of policy making in Western systems found its extension in evaluations of the applicability of such approaches to communist settings. So far, the results have been mixed. As regards the Soviet Union, it is perhaps a curious paradox that while the country is generally regarded as one of the most bureaucratised of the industrialised countries, the argument has been put forward, recently by Karen Dawisha, for instance, that the applicability of the bureaucratic politics model to the USSR is undermined by several factors, most notably the pervasive role of the Party in preventing bureaucratic conflict, and the influence of ideology in providing universal goals.[1] Similarly, Lucian Pye has written that the results of bureaucratic politics research in relation to China have been very slim and have provided little basis for a generalised understanding of Chinese politics.[2]

The contributions to the present volume tend towards the view that some suspension of disbelief might produce worthwhile results in specific areas and on specific questions. Both Marsh and Laux highlight the interplay between economic and political forces in the foreign policy orientations of the GDR and Romania. The 'primacy' of either, however, is not clear. Did the GDR enter the world market and new foreign economic relations and alignments as a means of achieving political and diplomatic objectives related to recognition? Or did these areas of goals compete with each other for political support, priorities and budgetary allocations? Or, for that matter, can the political goals to some extent be interpreted as means for the achievement of economic objectives? These kinds of questions cast some doubt on the wisdom of rejecting too quickly the utility of a perspective that would concentrate on competitiveness between bureaucracies in communist systems, as distinct from personal or factional conflicts within Party ranks.

Certainly, the top leaders of bureaucracies in communist countries are representatives of the Politburo or Central Committee in these organisations, but at the same time they and their own power are inextricably linked with the successes and failures of the organisations over which they preside. Rather than dismissing the relevance of the bureaucratic politics model altogether it may be better first to define precisely what is meant by it (there are widely differing definitions, even of one and the same author at differing points in time; Allison is a case in point); and then to pay due attention to what may be called the 'level of analysis' problem. Different bureaucracies, that is, may participate in the policy making process differently according to the kind and the type of decision at issue. Undoubtedly, the Ministry of Foreign Affairs, the Ministry of Foreign Trade, etc. will have a large role in the execution of day-to-day business and, together with the top representatives of the *institutchiki*, will be able to influence foreign policy making by virtue of the expertise they are able to offer. This may be true even for questions where policy is evolving in a long, drawn-out process. It will be less relevant in situations of international crisis, where a selected core of top leaders is more likely to proceed according to engrained 'operational principles' of behaviour and fall back on conditioned reflexes.

It is apparent from all of the countries discussed in this volume that the central directing role of the Party and its top leaders is not in question. Nor is the generally secondary nature of state or governmental institutions. What is in question, however, are the attitudes of individual groups, bureaucracies or institutions in the countries discussed, and the degree of influence they may exert in foreign policy making. There are some similarities between the various countries. The discussion in the chapters on the USSR and China concerning the Ministry of Foreign Affairs and, more generally, the foreign policy establishment in these countries, indicates that professionalisation and expertise is likely to produce policies different from those Party orthodoxy and Party *apparatchiki* would be prepared to admit. In both instances it appears also that the input of experts into the foreign policy process has been on a rising trend line. Nevertheless, the role of experts in foreign policy making in the countries examined has been — and most likely will continue to be in the near future — primarily a tool increasing the effectiveness of policy without challenging the overall objectives and directions set by the political leadership.

There are, however, considerable dissimilarities in the respective roles of the military — one of the several groups requiring more comparative attention than they have received hitherto. The internal political roles of the Soviet armed forces and the Chinese People's Liberation Army have been widely divergent. The contentious issues to which the relationship between the Party and the military gave rise in China from the early days of the communist movement have not been equalled in the Soviet Union. Use by Mao of the PLA during the Cultural Revolution to keep order while smashing vestiges of reaction and bureaucratisation within the Party, and directly involving the military in the internal administration of the country, were probably distinctively Chinese kinds of phenomena — and the same is true for the power that has at times been exerted by some of the regional military commanders. More recently the Chinese pattern again conforms more closely to the Soviet example, which, making due allowance for some exceptions as mentioned by Adomeit in the chapter on the USSR, is one of non-involvement of the military in political issues and readiness to accept the Party's leading role.

Differences in the relations between the military and political leadership in the two countries can be attributed in part to differences between Soviet and Chinese military doctrine, capabilities and technology, and between the kinds of operations they may be called upon to mount in war. In China, for example, statements in the late 1960s and early 1970s indicated expectations of future Sino-Soviet military conflict in which protracted 'people's war' would follow an initial Soviet strike. These were at the same time conditioned and stimulated by memories of the civil war period in China, and they had important implications for the role and standing of the PLA, reinforcing a traditionalist-oriented, ideological outlook on foreign and defence policies. In view of this legacy, it has not been an easy task for the political leadership to embark on the long overdue programmes of modernisation of the PLA, of which the import of Western military technology is a part. In contrast, in the Soviet Union a consensus has long existed between the political leadership and the military to the effect that military power is a precondition for exerting political influence abroad. Into this basic outlook fits neatly the high proportion of military expenditures in the Soviet GNP, the vigorous programmes adopted since Khrushchev's fall to achieve military-strategic parity (and thereby political equality) with the USA, as well as — more recently — the expansion of the roles of the Soviet Navy. It is for these reasons, among others, that it would be unwise to make too much of conflict between the Party and the military.

The chapters on Romania and China emphasise the role of ideology as a force of cohesion and integration, as well as mobilisation, in the domestic politics of these two countries. As for the importance of ideology in *foreign* policy making, careful distinctions need to be made. Combined with capabilities and political will in the Soviet case, it can be seen as a significant force shaping the Soviet interest in promoting and supporting political change outside its borders. In both the USSR and China, when contrasted with the exigencies of the moment, it has often given way to pragmatism and expediency. It does not follow from this, however, that it makes sense to draw rigid lines of irreconcilable conflict between 'pragmatism' on the one hand and 'ideology' on the other. Rigidity in doctrine does not rule out flexibility in tactics. (As elaborated by Adomeit in the chapter on the USSR, similar criticism must apply to the way in which some of the other traditional dichotomies have been developed, e.g. those between nationalism and ideology, and power and ideology.) Institutionalised in Party organs and personnel in the GDR, ideology had much to do with the criticism by conservatives of new emphases in the East German approach to foreign economic entanglements.

It could be argued that the changing agenda of international issues, including appreciation of commodity and energy resource needs, growing interdependence between the economies of Eastern and Western Europe, and demographic and other factors, could all combine to push ideology into a last-ditch defensive stand. But forecasts by Western analysts of the withering away and demise of ideology in communist systems, once economic problems have moved to a more satisfactory level of resolution, have been with us for almost as long as the communist systems themselves. Judging from all the contributions to this volume, the record of the 1960s and 1970s tends to reaffirm that tensions (rather than irreconcilable conflict) between pragmatism and ideology, nationalism and ideology, and power and ideology, are likely to continue in communist systems in one form or another and to influence foreign policy making. Ideology seems destined to remain as complex a concept as it has always been. Clearly, it plays some part in the shaping of goals, priorities and tactics; in shaping the perceptions and world views of communist leaderships, both universally and in relation to specific policy issues; in attenuating as well as exacerbating certain kinds of internal competition and conflict; and in structuring the domestic environment confronting communist policy makers.

Obviously, on this problem — as on the other problems dealt with — more thorough evaluation still needs to be done, and within such an endeavour comparison can serve a useful purpose. A number of similar criticisms and suggestions to that effect arose in each of the four country chapters. All the authors draw attention to the relative paucity of detailed and systematic investigation of communist countries' foreign policies. The chief reasons for this neglect in the East European cases have already been noted, particularly by Laux and Marsh with respect to Romania and the GDR: with the unambiguous exceptions of Romania, Yugoslavia and Albania, obedience to foreign policy directives from Moscow has seemed to Western observers to undermine the utility of treating each state as an entity. Neglect of more theoretical developments in foreign policy studies was likewise noted by each contributor, even where, as for example in the study of the USSR and China, students of domestic and comparative politics have for some time been making headway in the integration of communist area studies with the broader concerns of political scientists. Yet the degree to which recent research has departed from older norms of analysis — usually, if not always unambiguously, identified with the 'totalitarian' or 'bloc' model — and has begun to tackle group, linkage and other approaches to the study of foreign policy, is much in evidence throughout the book.

For the states of Eastern Europe, factors such as the Soviet presence, Communist Party linkages, geographical proximity, or shared historical experiences, point to the value of the observer engaging in more than occasional glances over the shoulder at what other countries within the regional subsystem are doing. Occasional glances, of course, have always been cast. Every traditional Kremlinologist worth his salt has moved in quickly on developments in one communist country which seemed to shed some light on events in another. The plea in the present contributions, however, appears to be for comparison to be sustained at more enduring levels, and for it to play a more fundamental role in guiding research goals and strategies than it has hitherto.

Comparison is too important to be left to the parentheses. Laux, for example, suggests at one point that in the case of Romania geopolitics cannot be taken as a major part of the explanation of the successful deviation of Bucharest from Moscow's line, since quite different stands in relation to the Soviet position on key foreign and defence policy issues have been taken by Hungary and Bulgaria, two states also located peripherally in relation to the Soviet presence in eastern Europe. In other words, if a particular factor, such as doctrine, is held to account for so much of a proportion of the foreign policy of country X in such-and-such circumstances, how is one to know, without comparison with countries A, B, C, and so on, and with other, quite different or quite similar, circumstances, whether the suggestion is to be regarded as 'normal' and expected, extraordinary, controversial, or trivial? The judgement of the individual scholar is an important part of the answer, but only a part. Too infrequently have interpretations of the sources of particular countries' policies been couched in terms that encourage observation and testing in others. This basic point applies also to the Soviet Union and China. In both instances, particularly perhaps the latter, the unique has been given undue emphasis. The distinctive features of each within the communist world are readily apparent: the USSR because of its sheer military might, visibility in world affairs, leadership role in the communist international system, 'special relationship' with the United States, technological superiority to other communist states, and other factors: China because of such considerations as its forging of a distinctive path to socialism, the blending of elements from antiquity and from modern Europe in the sinification of Marxism, and the peasant and guerrilla warfare origins of the communist movement with all the repercussions these have had on state and Party institutions and policy processes in the People's Republic. But, as the chapters on China and the Soviet Union have brought out, what dissimilarities there are between the two, or between either and other states in the communist world, need not be taken as barriers to useful comparative enquiry.

Some further examples might illustrate the point. Kuhlman has recently proposed a framework for analysing the domestic and foreign policy consequences of selected variables. The influence of trade dependency on policy, for example, could be studied by way of a comparison between Romania and Poland; the influence of the level of technology via comparison of the GDR and Romania; managerial expertise via Yugoslavia and Bulgaria; ideological orientation via Yugoslavia and Hungary; the CEMA role via the GDR and Yugoslavia; and ethnic homogeneity via Yugoslavia and Poland.[3] While this particular essay related only to the East European states, a similar procedure could be adopted on a larger scale. Thus the impact of variables related to traditional European culture, commonly cited in the literature on the Soviet Union and Eastern Europe, could with advantage be more systematically treated in comparisons with the Asian Party states. Aggregate cross-national research might allow conclusions to be drawn about the effects of size, levels of economic development, and other variables on communist foreign policies. Institutional variety, including contrasts in Party-state relations and differences in organisation, also suggests a potentially rich field of enquiry. Different degrees of openness to Western tourism or cultural values (between China and the GDR, for example) might facilitate the testing of some commonly cited propositions relating to détente in East-West relations. Transnational ethnic links and their implications for interstate relations (Albania-Yugoslavia, or China-Russia) have already been found to be worth further examination in the East European context. All the states in the communist international system offer opportunities for diachronic comparative analysis. In the present book, Laux noted its potential value for research on Romanian foreign policy. More thorough going treatments of the contrasts between the pre-revolutionary and communist periods would seem to be an indispensable mechanism for evaluating the continuing impact of classic foreign policy variables.

At the same time, however, we should not ignore some other questions. Both the chapters on the GDR and Romania in this book underline the significance of the small size of these two countries for their foreign policies. Ceausescu's own identification of Romania with the world of small powers — East, West and non-aligned — and their refusal 'any longer to play the role of pawns in the service of the interests of the big imperialist powers' might suggest a re-grouping of states habitually classed together. The point is underscored by Romania's labelling of itself in 1972 a 'less developed country', and by its role in UNCTAD from 1976. Similarly, though at a different end of the size range, China's repeated affirmation that it is not a superpower and, indeed, that the other states of the world should coalesce to oppose it should it ever show signs of becoming one, point to some benefit in re-classifying China into a Third World grouping. That is to say, delineating an academic field of comparative communist foreign policy studies might prejudge too many issues. It might predetermine which factors and which countries are likely to be concentrated on in research, and might conceivably therefore overlook a number of important questions.

The question of state typologies leads to the more immediately practical question of looking at the effects of and interconnection between different factors. Laux, for example, proposes the value of a comparative investigation that could link Romania with Belgium in a study of the foreign policy consequences of subordinate status in military alliance systems, or with Venezuela in research into state-directed industralisation policies. Other examples of useful comparisons with states outside the communist world can be cited — studies, for example, of the foreign policy implications of internal ethnic divisions (Cyprus or Belgium in contrast to Czechoslovakia or Yugoslavia), partition (Ireland compared with Korea and Germany), nuclear weapons technology (France and the Soviet Union, and/or China), economic penetration by alliance leaders (Italy and Bulgaria), and energy dependence (Denmark and Hungary).

All this does not mean that the efforts at comparing foreign policy making in communist countries should be abandoned before they have even begun in earnest. The proviso, however, is that the exercise of comparing communist foreign policies should not rest on faith in the distinctive characteristics alone of this group of states, nor rule out cross-cutting comparative perspectives.

This book, then, raises as many problems as it 'solves', and more than can be touched on in this brief concluding note. 'The comparative method', Rosenau has maintained, 'is but one of many ways of analysing foreign policy and it is not always the best way. Much depends on the researcher's purpose'.[4] With this qualified advocacy, the present authors are fully in agreement. They recognise a need for more, and not fewer, detailed case studies of foreign policy behaviour on the part of the communist states. An interest in comparative analysis is not inconsistent with variety in the approaches of different scholars. Comparative analysis carried out in a classical mould of international relations would produce different results from work carried out by a researcher committed to 'scientific' norms; but there is advantage in such diversity. Comparison, then, does not call for simple-minded rambles through the coincidental similarities of a complex world. Used with care, it is an indispensable tool for helping to identify those things that *are* unusual, idiosyncratic, or even — in the much-abused term of traditional communist studies — unique.

Notes

[1] Karen Dawisha, 'The Limits of the Bureaucratic Politics Model: Some Observations on the Soviet Case', Paper presented at the Annual Conference of the National Association for Soviet and East European Studies, Fitzwilliam College, Cambridge, 26-28 March 1977.

[2] Lucian W. Pye, 'Generational Politics in a Gerontocracy: The Chinese Succession Problem', *Current Scene*, XIV, 7 (July 1976), p. 9, n. 7.

[3] James A. Kuhlman, 'A Framework for Viewing Domestic and Foreign Policy Patterns', in Charles Gati, ed., *The International Politics of Eastern Europe* (New York: Praeger, 1976'), pp.278, 282 and 284.

[4] James N. Rosenau, 'Comparing Foreign Policies: Why, What, How', in id, (ed.) *Comparing Foreign Policies: Theories, Findings and Methods* (New York: John Wiley, 1974), p. 10.

Index